Heaven
and
The Believer

An Overview
of the
Future Events
for the
Church Age Believer

DR. ROBERT L. COURTNEY

Heaven and the Believer

Dr. Robert L. Courtney

© 2014, Tyndale Seminary Press
Hurst, TX

ISBN-10: 1-938484-15-0

ISBN-13: 978-1-938484-15-5

All rights reserved. No part of this publication may be reproduced, stored in a retrieval system, or transmitted in any form or by any means —electronic, mechanical, photocopy, recording, or any other — except for brief quotation in printed reviews, without the prior permission of the publisher.

**Scripture quotations taken from
the New American Standard Bible®,
Copyright © 1960, 1962, 1963, 1968, 1971, 1972, 1973,
1975, 1977, 1995 by The Lockman Foundation
Used by permission." (www.Lockman.org)**

Tyndale Seminary Press

Table of Contents

HEAVEN AND THE BELIEVER

Introduction	1
An Overview of the Future Events for the Church Age Believer	6

The Basic Facts of Heaven

Chapter 1 The Place Called Heaven	10
Chapter 2 The People of Heaven	16
Chapter 3 The Purpose of Heaven	21
Chapter 4 The Plan of Heaven	29

The Relationship of the Believer to Heaven

Chapter 5 The Believer and His Departure to Heaven	37
Chapter 6 The Believer and the Awards in Heaven	43
Chapter 7 The Believer and the Marriage of the Church in Heaven	49
Chapter 8 The Believer and the Second Coming of Christ	55
Chapter 9 The Believer and the Millennial Kingdom/Reign of Christ	67
Chapter 10 The Believer and the Great White Throne Judgment	75
Chapter 11 The Believer and the New Heaven and New Earth	81
Chapter 12 The Believer and Eternity	88

INTRODUCTION

I sit alone in my office and stare at the keyboard of my computer. A bright, white screen stares back at me, as if to say, "When are you going to get started?" I start my day in the same way you probably do. Some breakfast and a cup of coffee, then I settle into my favorite chair and spend some time reading the Bible and praying for my day, my children, my friends… I try to keep this routine, for I know what desires to occupy my time and thoughts. It doesn't take long for this very machine I type on to demand its portion of my day. Logging on, I find the need and desire to catch up on messages delivered to my email account during the night. No doubt some of the readers of this book will look back and think how archaic emails are. Yet, for the very reason that our world is in constant motion, change, even upheaval, I feel compelled to write out what lays on my heart. Following the news each day can be addicting. Story lines are set before me, calling me to return again to see what else has developed, convincing my mind that reality is what I see shining through this computer screen. Whether it is politics or disasters, the topics dominate our attention and our conversation. We know the reality of it. And as our communication system continues to evolve, our quest for 'knowing' remains. The instruments of transporting information do not quench the desire to have more.

Maybe I babble. Maybe I have lost your attention already. The media world may insist that there be a commercial interruption about at this point because our society can only take 'information' on one topic in small doses. I think you, my reader, may be different than the norm of information seekers. Just the fact that you are holding a book in your hand and reading it makes you different than some. That you have a desire to know about this topic will make you different too. I trust that it is not merely curiosity that has led you to follow the words I type. I do not write with this intention. The media of our day will cater to the desires and demands of its viewership. It will follow a prescribed course and mold its message around whatever principle drives it. We are conditioned that way. We scan through a couple of dozen topics on the news page, deciding which ones we are interested in and avoiding others.

At this moment, you have chosen to read this book. I do not know what has brought you my way, but I welcome you. We are about to explore a familiar topic. Even though it has been getting attention from folks like us about as long as the world has been, I think I have something to contribute to its study. But, I set before you the reality that I have never been to Heaven. I speak almost like a travel guide who describes a country they have never visited. In that, I do not have an "experience" to describe to you. I think it's fair, if you are taking the precious moments of your life to read what I write, that I tell you the reason for my writing and the method of my thinking.

First of all, I have never considered myself a book writer. I guess I don't mind pecking at a keyboard and producing lengthy volumes. My seminary professors received some rather long assignments over the years. Either I had much to say or I said too much. So, the mere task of putting together this book is not a concern to me. What has been my concern is what I have witnessed many times over the years. For every book, for every opinion stated, there are opposite opinions and critics. I do not doubt that there will be those who will work over this book, tear it apart, and find among other things the errors in spelling or grammar. I do not claim to have expertise in this area – just ask the dear lady who brought me a 3x5 card at the end of one of my sermons with a list of all the grammatical errors I made while preaching that day. Even beyond this, there are those who simply love to criticize and my writing will be a juicy target for them. Does it bother me – yes, somewhat. But I will get over it soon enough. I've seen what the theologians do with new works. I've seen the cautious approach, the critical eye, and the frown that reflects a difference of creed or position. Soon enough, I'll be placed in someone's 'theological box' and very likely you may find a copy of this work on the shelves of a thrift store. But, these things are not what cause me to hesitate as I stare at this screen again. My hesitancy concerns the reality that for every discussion at the Areopagus in Athens (Acts 17), there must be someone willing to go, to face the critics, and to boldly proclaim their message. Until recently, I have not desired to 'go.'

However, my dear friend and educational colleague, Dr. Chris Cone, of Tyndale Theological Seminary spent an afternoon with me pressing the value of writing down what one knows. Not for the sake of mere 'book writing' or even for popularity, but for the sake of those who need to know the truth. I doubt that I need to convince you that this world offers a lot of information that is not based on truth and is even contrary to the truth. I am no longer satisfied that my 'silence' is justifiable. Actually, it would be a disservice to you if I were to resist this any longer.

So, my motive is revealed. With all my heart and strength, I want to express to you the information I have, with the hopes that you will find it to be beneficial in your walk on this earth with the Lord. If it does not produce a measure of value – if it does not move you closer to some degree to our Savior – then the fault could be mine in poor communication – or it could be yours in the approach you have brought when you began to read. Don't be alarmed with such a statement. After all, neither of us are the measure of truth. We are the recipients of truth. God has spoken truth by His Word, the Bible. Errors are found among those who seek to handle it and understand it. Therefore, the method by which I seek to communicate to you must be carefully and faithfully employed. With that in mind, I set before you some of the principles that I hope I will retain throughout this book.

First, I believe that God's Word is true. We use theological words to express that in seminary. I choose to simply say to you that I am convinced that God has told us the truth. He did not leave it to opinions or hearsay, but recorded it by 'pen and ink' that we may have a lasting copy of His Word. It is my standard – all else is measured by it. Therefore, if I am going to write to you about Heaven, I do not need the 'experience' of having been there and back in order to present an authoritative statement about the place. It is sufficient for me that God has given us information about His Heaven in His Bible. I will elaborate more about this as I go on through this study. It is my hope that you will see it as 'principle one' in my book.

My second principle is that I believe that God never contradicts Himself. There are no passages in the Bible where God will state truth, then state the opposite as true also. No doubt some of you have just raised an eyebrow or in your mind started an argument against what I have just written. Let me be clear in stating that "IF" there appears to be a contradiction in the Scriptures, the problem does not lie with the truth of God's Word. The problem is with the reader who cannot put together in their limited mind that which can and must be understood only by the Spirit of God. Sometimes I find a difficult passage and I am prone to think that it may be speaking contrary to what I have read before.

Principle two reminds me that God's Word never contradicts itself. Therefore, it is my practice when I do not understand a passage, to start with the fact that if there is a problem here, the problem starts with me. I cannot trust my eyes and my mind – too often, that which I think I see is mixed together with my opinions, my perspectives and my notions. These are all influenced by the reality that I am a fallen person. My mind and perceptions are distorted by sin. My heart is deceitful. My desires are self-centered. In all this, reader, you have chosen to read the work of someone with serious limitations. So, don't be surprised at my second principle. Since God is true and what He says is true, then it is perfectly logical that He cannot and will not contradict Himself in His declaration of truth. Any errors of understanding rest with me and with you. My remedy is two-fold. First, I hold on tight to what I do know and readily confess what I do not know. The clear passages are my anchor in confusion. Second, I operate on the fact that trust must be an active part of all I encounter in the Bible. I trust what I do see and know. I trust what I cannot understand. Perhaps in due time, the Spirit will help me to grasp a passage that I cannot understand today. Perhaps He will find it more to my benefit to let me stay ignorant on the issue or passage and allow me to continue trusting that He has spoken truly. Personally, I am content with that. Knowing my limitations and His truthfulness gives me this principle that I hold on to dearly. I will do my best to be faithful to it throughout this book.

My third principle is found in the manner in which I will write. I desire to instruct you, encourage you, and exhort you from God's Word. I do not aim to express my opinion or my speculation. But should I do so, I will seek to be consistent and inform you, even forewarn you, that it is my opinion or speculation. I hope you find me true in this. I am not writing to entertain you or as I said earlier, to merely satisfy your curiosity. I feel the obligation to present what God has said, from His Word, to you in order that your faith may be strengthened and your understanding increased.

I should also say that as a pastor and professor, I am very concerned with protecting the Lord's "Sheep" from teaching that is contrary to truth. I write that you may discern truth and refute error. It is not my method to go after the teachings and books that teach inaccurately. Though, at times, it is necessary to bring something out to make the point. I am convinced that the answer to error is to present truth. The practice of writing books to counter other books creates an endless process and it wearies me even to read them. I have no desire to inflict that on you. To what extent I must bring out another's teaching or statements, I only do it that we may see the truth.

The topic is Heaven and the Believer. God has said much about it in His Word. My goal is to present what He has said in a logical and chronological manner. It will take a couple of chapters to establish the facts about Heaven and our relationship to it. Once we have settled that, I desire to walk you through God's plan for the Believer as it relates to His Heaven.

One may justly ask, "Don't we have enough books on Heaven?" Consider what is being read today about Heaven. Consider the number of things that are confused about Heaven. Consider the 'message' that is being presented today about who 'qualifies' to be in Heaven. If our answers are not coming from God's Word, then they are simply the reasoning of man. Having the word "Heaven" in the title does not mean that the message is a true one. I am convinced that the need for a clear statement on Heaven is necessary in light of the inaccurate information being distributed for the Church to digest. What I submit to you is as a humble servant of the Lord and student of His Word. As I open myself up to the critics, I only ask that you open your heart to His Word. Heaven is a place that we must know. It is a part of what God is doing. If we are not aware of it, how can we be prepared for it? D.L. Moody once said, "Heaven is a prepared place for a prepared people."[1] It is my desire to help you prepare.

---

[1] D.L. Moody, as quoted by George Sweeting, Compiled by George Sweeting, "*Great Quotes & Illustrations,*" Word, Incorporated, 1985, p. 135.

AN OVERVIEW OF THE FUTURE EVENTS
FOR THE CHURCH AGE BELIEVER

As I begin to specifically explain the future experiences of the Believer, I think it will be helpful to provide an overview of the events covered in this book. My goal is to produce a chronological viewpoint of what the Bible teaches about what we can expect. My focus is intentionally on the Church Age Believer.

Perhaps the first point ought to be a definition of the Church Age Believer. I purposely contrast this definition with that which would identify the Old Testament Saint, the Tribulational Saint, and the Millennial Saint. Without much explanation of the doctrine of this point until the chapter on "The People of Heaven," I simply write that the Church Age Believer is an individual who has put their trust in Jesus Christ for their salvation. The group of Church Age Believers begins on the Day of Pentecost as recorded in Acts 2, sometime around 33 AD. The Church Age includes all Believers in Christ from that day and throughout the history of the AD years until this present time. It will continue until the Rapture of the Church. Therefore, my definition of the Church Age is from the Day of Pentecost to the Rapture. It is the only time in history that the True Church will exist on this earth in its pre-glorified state. With that being expressed, I will now turn my attention to summarizing the future experiences of the Church Age Believer.

Departure

The first event for the Church Age Believer will be departure from this world. Like all who were before us, the possibility is great that our departure will be by death. For the Believer, "to be absent from the body is to be at home with the Lord" (2 Corinthians 5:8). That which may alter the manner of the Believer's departure is the Rapture of the Church. The reality is that every Church Age Believer will participate in the Rapture. For those who have already died, they will descend with Jesus in the clouds to be reunited with their glorified physical bodies. The Believers who are still alive on this earth, will be changed to glorified bodies and will join the Lord in the clouds. There, the True

Church will be united and will return with Jesus into Heaven. The details of and support for this departure will be explained more fully in a chapter to follow.

In the Present Heaven

The next set of events for the Church Age Believer will take place in the present Heaven. Many studies on eschatology spend a great portion of their time explaining the events that will take place on earth during the Tribulation Period. Though those events are described quite fully in Scripture, I will bypass them because they have no direct relationship with the Church Age Believer. During those seven years of Earth-side Tribulation, the Church Age Believer will be in Heaven.

The first event in the present Heaven, I believe, will be the Believer's judgment. This is typically called the "Bema Seat Judgment." It is not a judgment to see if the Believer belongs in Heaven, but it will be an evaluation of the service the Believer has rendered in the name of Jesus Christ. The Believer's works will be tested to reveal the true value and motives of that service. That which is pleasing to the Lord will be rewarded. That which is worthless will be consumed by the fire of His judgment. Primarily, this will be an awards ceremony, which will have its part in preparing the Church as the Bride of Christ for the marriage ceremony to follow.

After the Awards ceremony, the Church Age Believer will participate in the Marriage of the Lamb. The fact that Revelation 19 makes reference to it being already completed by the time the Lord returns in the Second Coming reveals that it must take place prior to that coming and after the Awards ceremony. Ephesians 5 gives us the description of Christ's love for His Bride, the Church. I understand the explanation to be something literal, not figurative, symbolic or allegorical. The simple fact is that the Church belongs to Christ and that will be fully realized in Heaven.

The Return

The next event following the Marriage of the Lamb will be the Second Coming of Christ to this earth. He is not coming as a humble baby this time, but as a warrior to rescue His people, the Jews who will be on the verge of extermination by the antichrist. The key principle about the Church Age Believer is that he will always be with the Lord (1 Thessalonians 4:17). When the Lord comes, then the Believers come with Him. The Church will not fight in the battle, but will be present and will see the Lord accomplish His promises and save His people.

Reigning with Him

Soon after His victory, the Lord will set up His 1000 year reign on this earth. It is theologically called the Millennial Kingdom. Jesus will literally sit upon the throne of David in Jerusalem and will rule over the whole earth for 1000 years. That too, is in keeping with His promises to His people, the Jews and the multitude of prophecies in the Bible. The Church Age Believer will be with Him and will sit on thrones reigning and serving as priests.

The Judgments

The Millennial Kingdom will come to an end and will be followed by a series of judgments. Revelation 20 describes the judgment of Satan, the destruction of the present earth and the present heavens, and the judgment of the unbeliever. The fact that the Church Age Believer will always be with the Lord assures that the Church will be present at these judgments. It does not mean that this will be a time of judgment on the Believer, but on the contrary, the presence of the Church at these judgments adds to the nature of them, especially in the sense that the Church will forever testify of God's grace and the difference it makes in a life. Believers will stand in stark contrast to their enemy, Satan, and to those who did not believe in Christ.

The New Heaven and Earth

The closing chapters of the Book of Revelation give a fascinating description of the New Heaven and Earth. Typically, when the present Heaven is explained, the characteristics of the New Heaven are used. In actuality, they are not the same place nor do they seem to have the same characteristics. Yet, it will be the New Heaven and Earth, along with the New Jerusalem, that will be the final and eternal home of the Church Age Believer.

CHAPTER 1
THE PLACE CALLED HEAVEN

As I stated in my introduction, the world has a desire 'to know.' It is amazing all that we have been able to discover through the technology of our day. The instruments that are used in these discoveries can work well with what is tangible and testable. But, how do you know what is not tangible or capable of being tested? In the nature of this book, how can we know that Heaven really exists? How do we know that what we have heard about Heaven is true?

These questions have been raised by so many, maybe even you and me. In the last handful of years, I have noticed an increase in the stories of those who have died for a short span of time and have returned to the earth – with a 'mission' and with a book to write. Honestly, it is not my desire to be cynical –especially since they are referencing "Heaven," a place I firmly believe to be real. However, since there are some who have gone public with their story, we are likely to hear what they say. There are also many who will base their hopes of Heaven on their message.

I had noticed recently, that a prominent news outlet had a video of a lady who had 'died' and was back now to tell her story and sell her book. As I scanned through the available videos in their archive, I noticed several stories, all similar in situation and outcome, yet varying from the experiences of a 4 yr old, to a middle-aged woman, to a medical doctor. There were at least six of these interviews between the dates of April 2011 and April 2013. Obviously there is a market for this. People want to know that Heaven really exists and the conclusion must be that if someone has been there and back, they know.

Should we accept their testimony? I would recommend that we employ a very important response. Let us put their word to the test. One thing we ought to learn from the early Church is that they evaluated the messages they received and measured them according to the truth. The Bereans were especially noted for their eagerness to receive the message and their practice of "examining the Scriptures daily *to see* whether these things were so" (Acts 17:11). John, the Apostle, encouraged the recipients of his letter to 'test the spirits to see whether they are from God, because many false prophets have gone out into the world" (1 John

4:1). In our 'politically-correct' world, is it permissible to do the same? Is it right for us to conclude that those who do not pass the test of Scripture are propagating a false message? I would answer that it is not only permissible for us to do so, but also that it is necessary that we do this for the sake of those who give attention and credence to their message. I believe we can argue all day whether they actually died or not or whether they entered Heaven or not. Such arguments are difficult to prove or counter. However, the test of their message is our safeguard in the truth. Since they are willing to state their message, we must be willing to test their message by the standard of truth we have been given in the Word of God.

For example, one medical doctor testified that he had died, went to Heaven, and has returned to tell us what he experienced. We tend to begin with trust, after all, he is a medical doctor and ought to know what 'dead' is. Since it is his practice to speak to patients about their actual conditions, we have a default setting to believe what he says. However, his testimony about the reality of Heaven was mixed with statements that he did not consider himself a believer in Heaven prior to his 'death' and that Hell does not exist. He was rather dogmatic on the last point.

Now, let us put on our discernment caps. We cannot do much about his experience except to listen with curiosity. His remark about his prior belief raises a couple of flags. Yet, his statement about Hell directly contradicts what the Bible teaches. Now, we are given a choice of which direction our trust will go. Shall we believe the medical doctor or the Word of God on this point? The Bible teaches about Hell in a very clear and authoritative manner. This man flatly denies what the Bible says. Either the Bible is all true, or it is not true. It cannot be true in some points and in error on others. The conclusion, based on the testimony of this man is that the Bible's teaching about the afterlife is not true and I guess we must believe that he was 'sent back' to correct it by his own experience. So, do we trust his message?

In another interview, a woman confessed openly that she was a sinner and an unbeliever (claiming that she had broken all of the Ten Commandments)... But after she died, she stood before God and He removed all her chains of sin and set her free from them. Then, of course, she was sent back with a message to help those who also struggle with the chains of sin. I would say initially that she has a worthwhile ministry if helping those in habitual sin is what she is called to do. Scripture teaches us to do this. However, I am compelled by the same Scripture to test the validity of her entire message. Her story included more than just the experience of being in Heaven; it also spoke of the issue of sin and forgiveness. In her own words, she received forgiveness and release from her 'chains of sin' after her death and when she stood before God. What that means is that she was not forgiven by the blood of Jesus Christ, but by another avenue. Actually, she made no reference to Jesus Christ at all (which is not uncommon in these stories). Her 'forgiveness' experience is contrary to the verse that says: "No man comes to the Father but through Me" (John 14:6). Should that be a big deal for us? Let us not forget that truth in Heaven issues is not separate from truth in salvation issues. If the Bible is not true in one part, it fails to be true in all parts.

Yet, a good portion of these 'death experiences' and the messages they bring are meant by those who tell their story to give us healing and hope. I ask, in keeping with the need for discernment, is this where we find our hope? Since when did the Bible become second place to the message and experiences of others? Can we really find more 'hope' and 'healing' in the words of someone who will contradict God's Word as they claim to relate God's message from Heaven?

I believe in a standard by which belief, experience, visions, revelations, whatever is expressed as truth to be believed, whatever is communicated to us as information, is to be measured. I am satisfied to place my faith and my hope in God's Word. As He tells me to, I will 'test the spirits to see whether they are from God, because many false prophets have gone out into the world."

Is it harsh to call these people 'false prophets?' Let me ask, do they have a message to tell? Have they made that message available to the public to hear and believe and find help on the topic of Heaven? Does their message contradict the teaching of God's Word? Will their message lead someone to believe them over what God has said? If the answer to these questions is "yes," then I also say "yes" to calling them false prophets.

My belief is that there is a Heaven and that there is sufficient material in God's Word about it. I've already confessed that I have never been to Heaven. I do not feel that I need to have been there in order to support my faith or to instruct you in yours. It is true that we are limited – trying to describe a place we have never been. But, that limitation is not a detriment – it is actually to our advantage.

The biggest need in the study of Heaven and the greatest result from it is in reference to our faith. We need faith strengthened, not replaced by the experiences of others. Our faith needs to keep growing. Our faith will be rewarded. As it was said of the saints in Hebrews 11:13-16,

> All these died in faith, without receiving the promises, but having seen them and having welcomed them from a distance, and having confessed that they were strangers and exiles on the earth. For those who say such things make it clear that they are seeking a country of their own. And indeed if they had been thinking of that *country* from which they went out, they would have had opportunity to return. But as it is, they desire a better *country,* that is, a heavenly one. Therefore God is not ashamed to be called their God; for He has prepared a city for them.

Who are we to counter their example of faith in God and the reality of Heaven?

When it comes to the topic of Heaven, who has greater authority to speak about it than God does? After all, He created it. To our benefit, He has chosen to tell us what we can know about it. I have heard some people quote from 1 Corinthians 2:9 ("but just as it is written, 'THINGS WHICH EYE HAS NOT SEEN AND EAR HAS NOT HEARD, AND *which* HAVE NOT ENTERED THE HEART OF MAN, ALL THAT GOD HAS PREPARED FOR THOSE WHO LOVE HIM'). They conclude from this that we cannot know about Heaven, since God hasn't shown it to us. Yet, as I have been reminded by one dear saint, that there is a verse which follows and states, "For to us God revealed *them* through the Spirit; for the Spirit searches all things, even the depths of God" (1 Corinthians 2:10). Therefore, let us see what God has said about the reality of Heaven.

Starting with the basics, there is much to God's description of Heaven. First of all, He tells us that the Heavens are more than just a single part. Throughout 2 Peter 3 (verses 7, 10, 12, 13) the term

'Heavens" appears in the plural. In 2 Corinthians 12:2, Paul speaks about the 'third' Heaven. From this we glean the fact that Heaven is described in the Bible on at least three levels. There is the first heaven, which is our atmospheric heaven. We typically call it our 'sky.' It is a place where the birds of the heavens fly (Genesis 1:20: "Then God said, '... let birds fly above the earth in the open expanse of the heavens"') and where we receive our rain (Deuteronomy 11:11, the rain of heaven)'. The Greek and Hebrew word for 'sky' is also the word translated as "heaven."

There is also the second heaven, which is the location of the sun, moon, stars, and planets. God told Abraham in Genesis 15:5 to "....look toward the heavens and count the stars...." Numerous other verses make reference to the 'stars of heaven.'

Our interest in this study is on the description of the third heaven. It is the dwelling place of God. When our Lord taught His disciples to pray, His first words were "Our Father, Who is in heaven...." (Matthew 6:9). This is probably the 'third' heaven Paul referenced in 2 Corinthians 12:2, a clearly identifiable place. In verse 4 of the same context, he identifies it as 'Paradise." The exact word used by Jesus when He promised the thief on the cross, "... Today you shall be with me in Paradise" (Luke 23:43). Wherever Jesus went after His death and with the thief, it was identified as Paradise. Hebrews 9:24 tells us that at His death, Jesus Christ entered the true holy place...."into heaven itself, now to appear in the presence of God for us." By putting together these pieces, we get a description of the third Heaven being the same as Paradise and the dwelling place of God. There is a place called "Heaven." It is the location where God is. It is the location where Jesus went (Ephesians 1:20). It is the place where God's throne is located (Isaiah 66:1 'Thus says the Lord, Heaven is my throne...'). From Heaven, God looks down on this world. He sees His people. He hears their prayers from Heaven. He made His plans from Heaven. This same place holds our spiritual blessings (Ephesians 1:3) and the place where we are actually 'seated' – a spiritual reality that will eventually become a physical reality (Ephesians 2:6). Heaven is so significant to the Believer that Ephesians 6:12 states that it is the location of the spiritual battles that concern us. Is there any wonder that Satan has chosen to attack our understanding of Heaven? It is to Satan's advantage that we become confused… that we doubt… that we let others in the world diminish its value, and strip down the gospel message, and rob us of the true nature of the place. You see, if we deny the existence of Heaven, We have contradicted God's message to us.

Put it this way, if there is no Heaven, then God has not told us the truth. If there is no Heaven, then He does not have a throne, and He is not overseeing the affairs of man. If there is no Heaven, then the thief on the cross went 'nowhere,' and Jesus went 'nowhere,' and the man in 2 Corinthians 12 went 'nowhere.' Then, according to Philippians 3:20: We who are believers are citizens of "nowhere." Our inheritance is nowhere. Our 'seat' is nowhere. Our battle is nowhere. Our hope is in 'nowhere.' Our future leads to 'nowhere.' Our faith is pointless.

Denying the existence of Heaven does more than just eliminate what cannot be proven in a laboratory, it has much greater ramifications: by denying the existence of Heaven, we state that the Bible is not true. We state that the gospel message is not true. You cannot separate these things without destroying them all. That's why I'm greatly concerned with the messages we get from the media. Oh, they promise a heaven, but it is built on political or spiritual 'correctness'. The message of the Heaven they proclaim is shaped by what man says and wants, and not based on what God has said. The fact that Heaven exists is not supported by the experience of man, but it is supported by the truth of Scripture. I belabor that point, I know. But the testimony of Scripture says that Heaven is a real place. It is a place Jesus has promised to those of us who will believe in Him. Since it is a place that I plan to be, I would rather trust Jesus with my eternity, than all the media and books written about those who have been there and have come back.

CHAPTER 2
THE PEOPLE OF HEAVEN

In the scope of this book, I will seek to explain what the Scriptures say about Heaven and the Believer. I think it would be best to begin with a more detailed definition of 'the Believer' than what I have already written in the "Overview" chapter. If a census were to be taken of the occupants of Heaven, it would certainly have to include God the Father, His Son Jesus Christ, and the Holy Spirit. It would also include the angelic host mentioned so often in the Bible. In addition to these, there will be the righteous ones of the Old Testament era, the saints of the Church Age, the saints of the Tribulation period, and the saints of the Millennial era. I will use the time span from the beginning of creation (Genesis 1) to the Day of Pentecost (Acts 2) to define the Old Testament era. The individuals of this era were given revelation by the Lord and were expected to trust Him by faith. Men like Abraham were considered righteous by means of faith (Romans 4:3-5). They did not have the privilege of knowing the sacrificial death of Christ on their behalf, but they trusted that God would justify the ungodly and believed in Him. In some regard, it is a more commendable faith than ours. At least we have the complete revelation in God's Word and the history of the cross of Christ on which to anchor our faith. They simply (and profoundly) had to trust the Lord. I admire their faith. Hebrews 11:16 states that God is not ashamed to be called their God and that God has prepared a city for them. Therefore, when we count the citizens of Heaven, we would certainly include the righteous of the Old Testament era.

This book primarily concerns the Believers in the Church era. The Church era began in Acts 2 (sometime around A.D. 33) and continues to the present day. I will spell out that era in the chapters to follow. For the purpose of this chapter, "The People of Heaven," I am addressing the saints of the Church Age. God's plan for them is uniquely designed, just as He has uniquely designed plans for the Old Testament saints, the Tribulational saints, and the Millennial saints. I will not be giving much emphasis to the last three groups, but will bring them into the picture as they correspond to the events of the Church Age Believer. Each one, especially the Tribulational and Millennial saints, would also be a fascinating study.

Years ago, D. L. Moody is reported to have said, "Heaven is a prepared place for a prepared people."[2] There is much emphasis in messages and books that Heaven is a prepared place. John 14:2 states it in Jesus' own words, "I go to prepare a place for you." But what about the second portion of Moody's statement? Is it 'for a prepared people?' Who are the people and how are they prepared? In our day of political correctness and all-inclusiveness, is it "fair" to say that it is 'for a prepared people' only?

If we were to talk to average people in this country, I am pretty sure we would find that the majority believe in Heaven. If we were to ask those who believe in Heaven about who its occupants will be, I am sure that we would find a great variety of answers. There are those who are sure that everyone will be there. There are those who believe our pets will be there. There are those who think that good people will be there but bad people will not. This idea has been promoted by the cartoon industry for years. It is not my desire to rehearse all the opinions of our present world's view of Heaven and who they say qualifies to be there. Suffice it to say, that as each day goes by, the Biblical teachings that we have held and still hold today, are becoming more unpopular. I do not think that is because we misunderstand what the Bible says, it is because the world does not like what the Bible is teaching. So, what shall we do? Should we soften our message so that the world may be pleased, or should we preach the Word so that some may be saved? If we are going to talk about Heaven, I think that it is right, that we also talk about how one gets there. As unpopular as this may be, I will first discuss those who won't be there.

Once a rich young ruler came to Jesus and asked Him what he should do to obtain eternal life. Perhaps he thought that being rich and being good were to his advantage. I think the world would agree with him. Yet, the interview ended with a disappointed rich young ruler, walking away after Jesus invited him to dispose of everything and follow Him.

On a previous occasion, Jesus addressed the crowd and spoke several things about those who gain eternal life and those who do not. In

---

[2] D.L. Moody, as quoted by George Sweeting, Compiled by George Sweeting, "Great Quotes & Illustrations", Word, Incorpora ed,

Matthew 7:13-23 Jesus spoke about two ways. In verse 13 He stated that there is a wide gate and a broad way. This gate is easily entered and the way is easily traveled. It is the preferred route for most people because it is easy. The gate and the way are not the end, but they both are part of the journey that leads to the end. Jesus said that the end of that journey is destruction. Unfortunately, He also said that there are many who follow this way.

In contrast, there is a small gate and a narrow way. The gate is not the easiest to enter. The way is not the easiest to travel. However, the destination is life. This marks a clear contrast between the two journeys and their destinations. The contrast is even shown in the participants. Many are on the road to destruction, but few are on the road to life. Here we have our first bit of information: the vast majority of the world will not be in heaven.

Observe a second fact Jesus taught in Matthew 7:21-22. There will be a group who will stand before Him someday in judgment. They will be seeking admittance into Heaven based on the works that they have done. They will say, "Did we not prophesy in Your name?" As if to say, doesn't proclaiming your message stamp our ticket? And 'Did we not cast out demons in Your name?" After all, we had a common enemy and proved we were on Your side. And, 'Did we not perform many miracles in Your name?" Surely, we did a lot of people a lot of good. Now, remember Lord, that we were careful to mention Your name each time we did something. That ought to count for something. Is it not a funny thing that we think we can manipulate the Lord into a corner and make Him respond in a way we desire? Of course, if we put the Lord's name on a plaque in a prominent place, He will bless our efforts, so we think. With all that free advertising, we ought to get free tickets, right?

Jesus responds in verse 23, "I never knew you." That is a significant statement. He did not say, "Oh, I didn't know you were doing this!" Rather, He stated that He didn't have any personal knowledge of *them*! He uses the Greek verb *ginosko*, which speaks of knowledge gained by experience. They shared no experience together. It wasn't a personal relationship. For those who were seeking admittance, it was merely business. Therefore, the principle is taught: you cannot earn entrance into Heaven, no matter how great your work or even if you tack

His name onto it. You cannot bargain your way into Heaven. On the positive side, those who do enter Heaven are those who have a personal relationship with Jesus Christ while they are here on this earth. Do you think it would be odd to invite a man to spend all of eternity with you when he spent no time with you on earth? How many times has a perfect stranger knocked on your door and you invited him to move in and live with you? So, what I gather, by the words of Jesus, and He ought to know, is that Heaven is not the place for the majority, Heaven is not a place to be bargained for, and Heaven is not a home for strangers to Him.

There are more verses that include a very descriptive list of those who are not Heaven's occupants. In Matthew 13:41-42, all those who are stumbling blocks and commit lawlessness are excluded. Their end will be in the Lake of Fire. In Matthew 13:49-50, the wicked are also cast into the Lake of Fire. There are many verses that follow this same pattern. Yet, to simplify the explanation, we can find teaching in Revelation 20:11-15 that identifies those who are excluded from Heaven. These are the participants in the Great White Throne Judgment. There we find the 'great' and the 'small' standing before the throne. They were judged by their works. They were also judged by the fact that their name was not found in the book of life. Regardless of their own importance or the nature of their works, without this designation in the book of life, they were cast into the Lake of Fire.

In the very next chapter of Revelation (21), there is a list given of those who will not be occupants of Heaven. Verse 8 states that the cowardly, unbelieving, abominable, murderers, immoral persons, sorcerers, idolaters, and liars will be cast into the Lake of Fire. Yet, there is more to this group. In John 3:36 it is said that 'he who does not obey the Son will not see life.' In a grand sweep, all those who practice sin (Romans 6:23), do not obey Jesus Christ, and have not put their faith in Him will be excluded from Heaven. The reality is that, apart from faith in Christ, no one qualifies for Heaven (Romans 3:23). The Bible is not silent about those who are excluded.

How then is Heaven a prepared place for a prepared people? What does the Bible say about those who will be in Heaven? The same verse quoted above (John 3:36) states that the one who believes in the Son has eternal life. John 3:16 says that "whosoever believes in Him… shall have everlasting life." John 1:12 states, "But as many as received

Him, to them He gave the right to become children of God, even to those who believe in His name." Jesus said, "No man comes to the Father but by Me" (John 14:6). Paul said, "Believe on the Lord Jesus Christ and you will be saved…" (Acts 16:31). Peter adds, "And there is salvation in no one else; for there is no other name under heaven that has been given among men by which we must be saved" (Acts 4:12). None of these verses speaks of earning entrance into Heaven and its eternal life. There is no bargaining. In fact, there is no qualification on the basis of the good one does or the bad one doesn't do. Heaven is not deserved. People will only be there because of belief in the Lord Jesus Christ. They will have received His mercy, grace and forgiveness. The Bible calls it a gift of grace simply because Jesus died the death that we deserved. He paid the price that we owed for our sin and could never repay. It is often said that Believers are simply sinners saved by grace. That is true. We cannot be 'prepared' for Heaven by our own doing. Rather, we are prepared by the nail-pierced hands of the Savior, Jesus Christ.

      The reality is, reader, that you will be either one who will be in Heaven or one who will not be in Heaven. The difference between the two ways involves your relationship with Jesus Christ. Can you say that you have your trust in Him for the saving of your soul? Those who can are those He has prepared for His prepared place. These are the Believers of the Church era.

CHAPTER 3
THE PURPOSE OF HEAVEN

There is a lot of curiosity about Heaven. That is quite understandable. There are many misconceptions about heaven too, and that is unfortunate. We have so much information in the Scriptures about it. Not only do the Scriptures tell us that it exists, but they also tell us why it exists. As eager as I am to describe Heaven to you, I think it is necessary to lay a proper foundation, which includes the purpose of Heaven.

By the time I was in elementary school, I was already a regular visitor at the eye doctor's office. In fact, my whole family was destined to keep the eye doctor well provided with customers. Perhaps you remember the device the eye doctor uses to adjust your vision. I was told that it is called a Phoropter. To me, it was a large black lens changer. You look through it and he says, "Is 1 better, or 2?" At the rate my eyes changed, it may have been cheaper to buy the Phoropter than the glasses. Obviously, I have a great dependence upon glasses and contact lenses.

There came a day in the 4th grade when the teachers were supposed to test the vision of all the students. We stood in a line at one end of the classroom and an 'eye-chart' was tacked to the bulletin board on the other side. When it came my turn to read the chart, they insisted that I take off my glasses and read the chart. I could not see a thing. There was a big black spot where the letter "E" was supposed to be. Later that day, I took home a note suggesting that I wear glasses. I do not recall how my parents received or responded to that note, but I do know that was the only time I had my vision tested at school. Every day since, I have been reminded of my dependence upon optical devices to keep my vision in focus. In a similar way, there is a need for us to be reminded that we must keep our focus on Heaven.

Colossians 3:1-4 states:

Therefore if you have been raised up with Christ, keep seeking the things above, where Christ is, seated at the right hand of God. Set your mind on the things above, not on the things that are on earth. For you have died and your life is hidden with Christ in

God. When Christ, who is our life, is revealed, then you also will be revealed with Him in glory.

The Apostle Paul is explaining why we must keep our focus on Jesus in Heaven. Before we dissect this passage, let us consider what we hear from some sources in history. It is not uncommon for the Believer to be criticized for believing in a place called Heaven. We have been told that it is a psychological crutch, a piece of our imagination, a myth, or a coping mechanism to help us deal with this world's challenges. Those who are supposed to be thinkers' in our world have bundled all our beliefs into a pile they simple call 'religion.' No doubt you are familiar with the words of Karl Marx about our beliefs: "Religion is the opium of the people." The quotation, in context, reads as follows (with my emphasis in bold and italics):

> The foundation of irreligious criticism is: Man makes religion, religion does not make man. Religion is, indeed, the self-consciousness and self-esteem of man ***who has either not yet won through to himself, or has already lost himself again***. But man is no abstract being squatting outside the world. Man is the world of man – state, society. This state and this society produce religion, which is an inverted consciousness of the world, because they are an inverted world. Religion is the general theory of this world, …its enthusiasm, its moral sanction, its solemn complement, and its universal basis of consolation and justification. It is the fantastic realization of the human essence ***since the human essence has not acquired any true reality***. The struggle against religion is, therefore, indirectly the struggle against that world whose spiritual aroma is religion.
>
> Religious suffering is, at one and the same time, the expression of real suffering and a protest against real suffering. *Religion is the sigh of the oppressed creature, the heart of a heartless world, and the soul of soulless conditions. It is the opium of the people.*
>
> The abolition of religion as the (misleading) happiness of the people is the demand for their real happiness. To call on them to give up their illusions about their condition is to call on them to give up a condition that requires illusions. The criticism of

religion is, therefore, in embryo, the criticism of that vale of tears of which religion is the halo. Criticism has plucked the imaginary flowers on the chain not in order that man shall continue to bear that chain without fantasy or consolation, but so that he shall throw off the chain and pluck the living flower.[3]

By equating our beliefs to opium, we can conclude that Marx saw religion as a device for irritating, numbing, and calming our pain caused by our weakness. Within four years, this message had made its way into the Church. Charles Kingsley, of the Church of England, wrote, "We have used the Bible as if it were a mere special constable's handbook, an opium dose for keeping beasts of burden patient while they were being overloaded, a mere book to keep the poor in order."[4]

Later, the architect of the Soviet state and founder of the Russian Communist Party, Valdimir Lenin stated,

> Religion is one of the forms of spiritual oppression which everywhere weighs down heavily upon the masses of the people, over burdened by their perpetual work for others, by want and isolation. Impotence of the exploited classes in their struggle against the exploiters just as inevitably gives rise to the belief in a better life after death as impotence of the savage in his battle with nature gives rise to belief in gods, devils, miracles, and the like. Those who toil and live in want all their lives are taught by religion to be submissive and patient while here on earth, and to take comfort in the hope of a heavenly reward. But those who live by the labor of others are taught by religion to practice charity while on earth, thus offering them a very cheap way of justifying their entire existence as exploiters and selling them at a moderate price tickets to well-being in heaven. *Religion is opium for the*

---

[3] Marx, Karl, *A Contribution to the Critique of Hegel's Philosophy of Right*, Introduction, first published in *Deutsch-Französische Jahrbücher*, 7 & 10 February 1844 in Paris, translation corrected by Andy Blunden, February 2005, and corrected by Matthew Carmody in 2009,
http://www.marxists.org/archive/marx/works/1843/critique-hpr/intro.htm
[4] As quoted by Brad Chilcott, *Get Off the Opium*, Posted Apr 4 2013,
http://www.redletterchristians.org/get-off-the-opium/

people. Religion is a sort of spiritual booze, in which the slaves of capital drown their human image, their demand for a life more or less worthy of man.[5]

Based on these quotes, our belief in Heaven is a drug or an alcoholic beverage and is meant to keep us in a stupor since we are too weak to live in the world of man. In order to cope, we must imagine a better place for us to go. Heaven's existence is merely the imagination of man.

However, the teaching of the Bible has a different thing to say about the purpose of Heaven. First, we see that in the very beginning of time, God had the existence of heaven recorded, "In the beginning God created *the heavens* and the earth" (Genesis 1:1, my emphasis). Why did God create two places, the heavens and the earth? Why not just one place? There must be a purpose.

As John began to write his Gospel, he recorded these words: "In the beginning was the Word [Jesus Christ], and the Word was with God, and the Word was God. He was in the beginning with God. ***All things came into being through Him, and apart from Him nothing came into being that has come into being***" (John 1:1-3, my emphasis). No doubt, you can see that I have inserted and identified "the Word" as Jesus Christ. That is John's argument as well in his first chapter. Clearly, Jesus Christ must be included in the conversation. He was instrumental in the creation of everything, including Heaven.

When Paul wrote his letter to the Colossians, he stated,

> He (Jesus Christ, inserted from the context of verse 13) is the image of the invisible God, the firstborn of all creation. For by Him all things were created, *both* in the heavens and on earth, visible and invisible, whether thrones or dominions or rulers or

---

[5] Lenin, Vladimir, from an article, *Socialism and Religion*, Published: Novaya Zhizn, No. 28, December 3, 1905. Signed: N. Lenin. Published according to the text in Novaya Zhizn, *Lenin Collected Works*, Progress Publishers, 1965, Moscow, Volume 10, pages 83-87, transcribed by B. Baggins, credited to the "Marxists Internet Archive." http://www.marxists.org/archive/lenin/works/1905/dec/03.htm

authorities--all things have been created through Him and for Him (Colossians 1:15-16).

What do we see in these verses? First, all things (including Heaven) were created *through Him*, that is, by His own activity. Second, all things (including Heaven) were created *for Him*. Here is the purpose for Heaven's creation: it was created FOR HIM.

This means that the heavens, the earth, even the whole universe is a Christo-centric universe. We think that gravity holds it all together, but Jesus holds even the gravity together as verse 17 adds, "He is before all things, and in Him all things hold together."

Here are a few observations. First, Heaven was God's idea, not a creation of our own imagination. Second, Heaven's primary purpose is not centered on you or me. Rather, it is centered on Jesus Christ.

Maybe we share the same problem. At times, I start to think that I am the center of this universe. I think and speak about "my life..... my time.... my way... my opinion.... my job..... my family." Take a survey of how often you use the pronouns "I," "Me," or "My" in a day's time; then ask yourself, "Who is the center of my universe?" The point I am making is this: Was Heaven created for a purpose? Yes, I believe it was. Is its main purpose 'man-centered?' No, that is not the teaching of Scripture. As we have just seen, Colossians 1:16 says that it was created FOR HIM (Jesus Christ).

Ephesians 1:10 and 12 says the same thing about the grand purpose and future time when all things will be gathered together and summed up. Specifically, the 'things in the heavens and things on the earth" which includes the 'all things' that He has created will be summed up in Christ. That includes you and me. Verse 12 adds the purpose, "to the end that we who were the first to hope in Christ **WOULD BE TO THE PRAISE OF HIS GLORY"** (my emphasis). Even the first song recorded in the Book of Revelation has the words, "Thou art worthy, O Lord, to receive glory and honor and power: for thou hast created all things, *and for thy pleasure they are and were created*" (Revelation 4:11, my emphasis).

What can we gather from this? THE PRIMARY PURPOSE FOR THE CREATION OF HEAVEN IS TO THE PRAISE OF HIS GLORY. Is it any wonder that the world would criticize us for our beliefs in

Heaven? They do not want to recognize Jesus Christ and give Him glory. They somehow think that by erasing Heaven, they have erased any accountability they have to Jesus Christ, and therefore have no reason to hold to His existence. However, they are in fact wrong. Unfortunately, to some degree, we give some leverage to their rants by placing ourselves as the most important aspect of this world and by suggesting, at least unconsciously, that heaven exists because of us.

Now is a good time for a 'Spiritual Phoropter.' It is time to reset our focus. By reviewing Colossians 3:1-4, we see that we have a different purpose to declare. The first comment, "Therefore if you have been raised up with Christ" brings up the definition of a Christian. A Christian is one who has been 'buried with Christ and has been raised up with Christ' (Romans 6). The 'if' in the early part of the statement is better expressed "since." We do not start with any doubt, but with a firm platform - "Since we have been raised up with Christ…." Based on that reality, we "keep seeking the things above." It is important that believers keep a heavenly focus. In fact, it is so important that we are commanded to do so. The Greek parsing of this verb reveals several vital points. It is identified as a '2nd Person, Plural, Present, Active, Imperative.' Being '2nd Person' means "you." That makes it personal. "You keep seeking things above." Being 'plural' means "you all" and therefore no believer is exempt or omitted. "All of you keep seeking things above." Being 'present' means 'Don't stop." 'All of you keep on seeking things above." Being 'Active voice' means that the subject (you) is doing the action. The action is not done for you. Nobody else is responsible for what you are supposed to be doing. "All of you are to keep on seeking things above." Being 'Imperative' means that it is a command, not a suggestion and not an option. Either we are seeking or we are not. If not, then we are being disobedient. The force of these words changes the whole focus on the purpose of Heaven from the puny Christian's way out to the obedient Christian who has set his mind on things above. If nothing else, we can consider any opposition to our focus on Heaven to be an attempt to get us to disobey our God.

Much more is included in these Colossian verses. It is not merely 'things above' that keep our focus, but "***WHERE CHRIST IS***, seated at the right hand of God" (Colossians 3:1, my emphasis). Our Savior lived in eternity past in this Heaven we talk about. At a particular point in

time, He took on human flesh, lived among men on this earth, and died on a cross for our sins. He was buried, and rose again the third day, according to the Scriptures. He then ascended into Heaven and seated Himself at the right hand of God. Not only has He created Heaven for His own glory, but He also is the centerpiece of Heaven. Put it this way, Heaven exists for the purpose of showing the glory of and prompting the worship of our Savior, Jesus Christ.

As if we need it restated, Colossians 3:2 says, "Set your mind on the things above, not on the things that are on earth." This is a little more potent than what we simply see. He calls for us to intensely set our interest (our affections and our thoughts) on the things above.   A. T. Robertson reminds us that, 'It does matter what we think and we are responsible for our thoughts.'[6] If our thoughts are centered on this world, we will think like this world, talk like this world, plan like this world, and behave like this world. Simply put, we will believe in this world. However, if our thoughts are centered on Christ, we will think like Christ, talk like Christ, plan like Christ, and behave like Christ. We will clearly show that we believe in Christ.

Heaven is God's creation. It was created for His purpose, His pleasure, and His glory. Heaven is where He is. That is why we are commanded to think on Heaven and on our Savior who is there. In addition to this, Colossians 3 adds one more aspect that ought to keep our thoughts riveted on things above. Paul writes in verses 3 and 4, "For you have died and your life is hidden with Christ in God. When Christ, who is our life, is revealed, then you also will be revealed **with Him in glory**" (my emphasis). This Jesus, whom we adore, worship and praise, deserves the glory because of Who He is. However, we as Believers know that He also receives the glory for what He has done. What is amazing is that He intends to share Heaven with us who believe in Him. One of my favorite passages is John 14:1-3. There, Jesus said,

> Do not let your heart be troubled; believe in God, believe also in Me. In My Father's house are many dwelling places; if it were not so, I would have told you; for I go to prepare a place for you.

---

[6] Robertson, A. T., Word Pictures, Word Pictures in the New Testament, e-Sword, Version 10.1.0, Copyright 2000-2012, Rick M

> If I go and prepare a place for you, I will come again and receive you to Myself, that ***where I am, there you may be also*** (my emphasis).

This is another reason why Heaven exists. Heaven exists as a place where Believers in Christ will be with Jesus. How often we find these words in the Bible! For example, "Then we who are alive and remain will be caught up together with them in the clouds to meet the Lord in the air, and ***so we shall always be with the Lord***" (1 Thess. 4:17, my emphasis). And,

> For to me, to live is Christ and to die is gain. But if *I am* to live *on* in the flesh, this *will mean* fruitful labor for me; and I do not know which to choose. But I am hard-pressed from both *directions,* having the desire to depart ***and be with Christ***, for *that* is very much better (Philippians 1:21-23, my emphasis).

And one of my favorites, 'We are of good courage, I say, and prefer rather to be absent from the body and ***to be at home with the Lord***" (2 Corinthians 5:8, my emphasis).

Just think of the wisdom of the teaching of Heaven. Some people live as if this life is all there is. If they have a difficult life, they may easily think that somehow they were 'ripped off' and ought to get a second chance at it. I would think that if our attentions were on this world only, we would be among the most miserable people on earth. However, God in His wisdom tells us in His Word of the place He has created. It is the place where He and Our Savior dwell. He lifts our eyes up and He invites us to share that Heaven with Him. We can carry on because we believe in that place. It has a purpose in our faith. It is the focus of our eyes. It is the hope of our soul. It is the place where we will be with Jesus.

CHAPTER 4
THE PLAN OF HEAVEN

We are living in a fascinating time. Who would have thought that we would be able to visit places all over the world through GPS systems, satellites, and internet programs without leaving our desktop computers? I have never been to such places as the Taj Mahal, the Great Wall of China, or the Eiffel Tower, but I have enjoyed them right from my living room. Certainly, it is not the same as being there, but technology allows us to have a few of these places we would not otherwise have.

Imagine how popular it would be if our technology allowed us to get a satellite image of Heaven. How wonderful to be able to follow its roads and view its landmarks. I have no doubt that if such a thing was possible; we would seek to enhance it with live video as well. However, as much as we might dream about it being so, the reality is that the only information we have concerning the description of Heaven is in the authoritative Word of God. One important thing to note is that this reality is not a limitation. It is a reminder that God's Word is sufficient for our need. It is our counselor, our guide, our encourager, our corrector and our source of information. I have met those who have believed that they needed more than what the Bible has to offer. They count on philosophies and opinions of other men and the use of their own wisdom. But, the best that the world has to offer comes from a fallen position - from minds that have been marred by sin and are depraved and limited. That is the best I can offer you too, if all I offer you are my opinions. You can choose which one you prefer to trust. I have made my choice, and that is the reason I write to you not about my opinions, but about the truths found in God's Word.

I repeat that what we learn from the Bible about the subject of Heaven is not limiting to us. It is faith building. Do we trust that what God has said is true and that it is sufficient? We have already seen that the Bible teaches that Heaven does exist. We have seen that Heaven is a prepared place for a prepared people and only those who have placed their trust in Jesus Christ will find their names in the Book of Life. We have seen that Heaven exists for a purpose. In this chapter, I want to look through Scripture again and map out what God tells us about His plans for Heaven.

In reality, this is a topic we should hesitate to approach, especially if we do not approach it with an attitude of respect, fear, and awe. Anytime we enter into the planning room of the Lord, we ought to approach with the greatest of caution. Far too often we assert our own wisdom and conclude that we have it all figured out, that we understand the ways of God, and that we comprehend 'why He does, what He does.' I am reminded of Job and his conversation with God, beginning in Job 38 and following for several chapters. Up to that moment and through the rest of the book of Job, we find Job slowly opening his peacock feathers and speaking as if he knew how God operates. Then God speaks, and among His first words to Job were, "Where were you when I laid the foundations of the earth?" (verse 4). Perhaps it is as if He said, "Job, I could have used your wisdom!" Consider the wise choice of God to make man on the last day of creation instead of the first. Even the timing suggests that God did not need anyone to advise or assist Him, nor does He need anyone to defend His plans. Proverbs 3:19 states, "The LORD by wisdom founded the earth, by understanding He established the heavens." Isaiah adds, "For My thoughts are not your thoughts, Nor are your ways My ways, declares the LORD. For *as* the heavens are higher than the earth, so are My ways higher than your ways and My thoughts than your thoughts" (Isaiah 55:8-9). These verses simply introduce to us the fact that the creation of the Heavens came about in the wisdom of God. At some point in eternity past, God mapped out His plan for Heaven – where it would be, what it would be, when it should be, when it should not be, and when another would stand in its place. And that God wanted us to know about His great plan; He has told us in His Word.

Let us follow the plan from the beginning of creation. God, at a particular time, created the Heavens. "In the beginning God created the heavens and the earth" (Genesis 1:1). That is not merely a memory verse. It is a statement of Heaven's origin. At some point, when Heaven did not exist (as hard as that might be to comprehend), God created it. Heaven has a beginning and is not eternal, as some would think.

I believe there are several reasons this information is important. First of all, God is not dependent upon Heaven for His existence. He is perfectly able to get along without it, as He did before Heaven was created. Secondly, in a theological way, you can loosen your grip a bit on heaven. Heaven is not God. God is God, and Heaven is His creation. He created it. I have been told that the word 'create' is only linked with God in Scripture, as if to say that creation is only His department. We understand this to mean that He does not need pre-existing material to start His projects. He creates out of nothing.

Man, on the other hand, is much like the music composer. We often identify the author of a musical piece as the arranger. That is the best that we can do. The notes already exist. We just shuffle them around on the page and form a different tune. Man does not create. He just arranges what has already been created. God is the creator. He did not borrow from someone else's ideas nor did He need supplies and materials from the lumber yard. I know that is a big concept, but as we have learned, "By faith we understand that the worlds were prepared by the word of God, so that what is seen was not made out of things which are visible" (Hebrews 11:3). Is it beyond our faith to believe that God created Heaven, that it has a beginning place in God's plan and exists at His pleasure or even His disposal? He is not dependent upon it, but it is dependent upon Him. These things are the first things we understand about God's plan for Heaven.

In moving on with His plans, I think it is good for us to understand that when God finished the creation of the present Heaven, He did not need to keep working on it. When He completed His creation the Scripture says, "God saw all that He had made… And behold it was very good…" (Genesis 1:31). The next chapter in Genesis begins, "Thus, the heavens and the earth were completed…" (Genesis 2:1). The verb 'completed' signifies 'at an end, finished, and accomplished.' What can we conclude from these two verses? First, we see that when God created the present Heaven, He also completed it. Second, that if He created it, it has a purpose in His plan. As far as we can surmise, at least part of that purpose is to give us a place to identify as God's place. As I have written earlier, God is not dependent upon Heaven, but He chose to create a place that we would identify as His abode. Without such a place, I think we would have a hard time with the fact that He is omnipresent. Heaven is not meant to limit that truth at all, but to give us a focal point in our understanding about God. Colossians 3:1, for example, tells us to "keep seeking the things above, where Christ is, seated at the right hand of God." It would be hard for us to mentally seek things above if such a place did not exist. So, for our limited minds, God has chosen to create Heaven as a place where He is. Thus, we have learned to say, 'Our Father, who art in Heaven." We read, 'the God of Heaven" and 'the Lord looks down from Heaven." We understand that it is a place that He has chosen to identify as His home, even though it is inadequate for His dwelling place. Solomon reminds us that Heaven and the highest Heaven cannot contain Him (1 Kings 8:27). Yet, it does us good to think of Heaven as His home.

Related to this, we also speak often about the throne of God. Scripture identifies the location of God's throne in Heaven. The relatively unknown prophet Micaiah said, "Therefore, hear the word of the LORD. I saw the LORD sitting on His throne, and all the host of heaven standing by Him on His right and on His left" (1 Kings 22:19). It is interesting to note that we can trace our way through the Bible and it is not until we enter the time of David's kingdom that we begin to associate God with a throne. Psalm 9:4 states, "For You have maintained my just cause; You have sat on the throne judging righteously." Verse 7 adds, "But the LORD abides forever; He has established His throne for judgment." Psalm 11:4 definitely states, "The LORD is in His holy temple; the LORD'S throne is in heaven; His eyes behold, His eyelids test the sons of men" and Psalm 45:6 declares, "Your throne, O God, is forever and ever; A scepter of uprightness is the scepter of Your kingdom." Many other verses in the Psalms record the same fact.

Another thing to note is that God's throne in Heaven was from the earliest time we conceive of Heaven's existence. Sometime in the past, Satan desired to set up a throne in Heaven, when he said, "I will ascend to heaven; I will raise my throne above the stars of God, And I will sit on the mount of assembly In the recesses of the north. I will ascend above the heights of the clouds; I will make myself like the Most High" (Isaiah 14:13-14). While it is difficult to pinpoint the exact time Heaven came into existence or when God's throne was established in it, clearly the Bible does not consider His throne merely an item of history. The fact is that His throne still exists in Heaven. The Hebrew writer often mentions it. Hebrews 4:16 reads, "Therefore let us draw near with confidence to the throne of grace, so that we may receive mercy and find grace to help in time of need." Hebrews 8:1 reads, "Now the main point in what has been said *is this:* we have such a high priest, who has taken His seat at the right hand of the throne of the Majesty in the heavens." Hebrews 12:2 reads, "fixing our eyes on Jesus, the author and perfecter of faith, who for the joy set before Him endured the cross, despising the shame, and has sat down at the right hand of the throne of God." Besides all this, the Book of Revelation has more information in it about the throne of God than any other book in all of Scripture. Clearly, it is understood, that God has a throne in Heaven.

In addition to a throne, we are given the information that Heaven also contains a temple. One of my favorite verses is found in Isaiah 6:1. There Isaiah records what he sees. "In the year of King Uzziah's death I saw the Lord sitting on a throne, lofty and exalted, with the train of His robe filling the temple." Though we are aware of the existence of a temple on earth in the days of Solomon, and another temple in the days of Christ, we can easily overlook the fact that a temple exists in Heaven. In which temple did Isaiah see the Lord? It might have been the temple that existed in his day. That would be impressive indeed to see the Seraphim circling around the throne as the Lord sat in the temple. However, we cannot simply conclude that Isaiah was seeing an earthly temple. According to Hebrews 8:5, Moses was to make the tabernacle according to a pattern shown to him. Hebrews 9:11 adds that Christ entered through a greater and more perfect tabernacle that was not made with hands nor was it of this creation. Then, as if to make it quite clear, the writer adds in 9:24, "For Christ did not enter a holy place made with hands, a *mere* copy of the true one, but into heaven itself, now to appear in the presence of God for us." Ample verses follow in Revelation that repeat the truth, "and the temple of God which is in heaven was opened" (Revelation 11:19).

It would appear that from the very beginning of the creation of Heaven, God's plan included Heaven to exist as His abode and to be the location of His throne and temple. This Heaven still exists as He has so designed, but it is not meant to remain that way.

For some, it is not desirable to consider that God plans to replace the current Heaven. Over the years, a sloppy approach has been used to teach about heaven and many have rested heavily upon those things. As a result, there are misunderstandings, especially in the plans God has for the future of Heaven. Yet the truth remains, the present Heaven is only meant to be temporary. For years, many have viewed it as the location where their mansion is being built, where the streets are made with pure gold, and where they will spend all of eternity. It is hard to conceive that this so-called mansion will be torn down and replaced. Yet, the words of the Scriptures make it clear that the existing Heaven will someday be destroyed and replaced with a new and eternal Heaven.

Peter is quick to tell us that the destruction of the present Heaven is according to a promise:

> But by His word the present heavens and earth are being reserved for fire, kept for the day of judgment and destruction of ungodly men. But do not let this one *fact* escape your notice, beloved, that with the Lord one day is like a thousand years, and a thousand years like one day. The Lord is not slow about His promise, as some count slowness, but is patient toward you, not wishing for any to perish but for all to come to repentance. But the day of the Lord will come like a thief, in which the heavens will pass away with a roar and the elements will be destroyed with intense heat, and the earth and its works will be burned up (2 Peter 3:7-10).

Twice Peter emphatically states that this judgment will involve both the Earth and the Heavens. The promise is in keeping with what Isaiah wrote long before, "For behold, I create new heavens and a new earth; And the former things will not be remembered or come to mind" (Isaiah 65:17). John would later record, "Then I saw a new heaven and a new earth; for the first heaven and the first earth passed away, and there is no longer *any* sea" (Revelation 21:1). The information is consistent throughout Scripture – the present Heaven will be destroyed and a new Heaven will replace it. "'For just as the new heavens and the new earth which I make will endure before Me,' declares the LORD, 'So your offspring and your name will endure'" (Isaiah 66:22). It may be hard, but we should loosen our grip on the present heaven. From all that I can see explained to us, the present Heaven is considered a resting place along the way for us.

The classic passage we cite when we talk about Heaven is found in John 14. There Jesus tells His disciples, "In My Father's house are many dwelling places; if it were not so, I would have told you; for I go to prepare a place for you" (14:2). A couple of key points can be made that would help us to understand this passage. First, Jesus promised to go and 'prepare' the place for them. The fact is, the place already exists. He had just said, "In My Father's house are many dwelling places." They already exist. The fact that He is preparing them speaks not of creation but of making them ready according to the idea of arranging things before a traveler arrives. The "dwelling places" or rooms are quite a bit different than the concept that we each will have our own mansion. Even the term 'mansion' suggests something quite different from what we generally conceive. The word does not mean exactly what we envision as a Victorian Mansion or a European Castle. The word mansion is derived from the Latin and speaks of a place to rest – merely a stop along a journey. In our present understanding, it would be equated more with a motel than with a castle. By this, I do not intend to minimize what the Lord is preparing for us, I know that all He does is grand and will far surpass all that we can possibly conceive down here. However, such an understanding fits better with what Jesus promised, especially since He knew the plans for the future Heaven. He never said, "If I go and prepare a place for you, I will come again and receive you to myself, so that you may live forever in that place…" Rather, He did say, "If I go and prepare a place for you, I will come again and receive you to Myself, that where I am, *there* you may be also" (John 14:3). Several things are clear. The place that currently exists is a single house with many rooms to rest in along the journey. Secondly, the promise is all about us being with Him wherever He is, not merely us being in this Heaven forever. The following chapters will say more about this, but the fact is that when we leave this earth at death or the rapture of the Church, we shall go to be with Jesus where He is. 1 Thessalonians 4:17 states, "Then we who are alive and remain will be caught up together with them in the clouds to meet the Lord in the air, and so we shall always be with the Lord." In 2 Corinthians Paul adds, "we are of good courage, I say, and prefer rather to be absent from the body and to be at home with the Lord" (5:8). We will find that when Christ returns to the Earth to reign in Jerusalem for 1000 years, we will come with Him. When the present Heaven and Earth are destroyed, we will be with Him. When the New Heaven and Earth are created, we will be with Him. Our future is anchored in Him, not in the present Heaven.

It is in His plan to destroy the present Heaven and to replace it with a new and eternal Heaven. There will be a throne in the New Heaven. One of the first things said about it is, "And I heard a loud voice from the throne, saying, 'Behold, the tabernacle of God is among men, and He will dwell among them, and they shall be His people, and God Himself will be among them'" (Revelation 21:3). However, there will be a change in regard to the temple. John makes this observation, "I saw no temple in it, for the Lord God the Almighty and the Lamb are its temple" (Revelation 21:22). We will discuss the details of this magnificent place in a future chapter.

While there is much more yet to learn, we now have a view of God's plan for Heaven. I find it both exciting and humbling that this plan has been so carefully designed to include those of us who believe in the Lord Jesus Christ. I suppose that we would be content to spend eternity with Him in any location, however what a wonderful expression of the Believer who contemplates all that Christ has done for us and exclaims, "All this, and Heaven too!"

CHAPTER 5
THE BELIEVER AND HIS DEPARTURE TO HEAVEN

Several chapters ago I discussed the question of who will be in Heaven. At that time, I chose to be specific about one particular group of heavenly occupants, Believers in Jesus Christ. I choose to focus on this select group because it is my hope that you are included in it. In our present day there are only two groups on the earth, Believers in Jesus Christ and those who do not believe in Him. Those who believe in Him are those who will go to the Father in Heaven according to John 14:6 as Jesus said "….no man comes to the Father but through Me."

Yet to be accurate, our current time period is not the only time period to consider concerning those in Heaven. The select group of Church Age Believers are not the only occupants of Heaven. To be specific, the Scriptures make it clear that Heaven is occupied by a host of angelic beings. The class of angels is made up of Seraphim, Cherubim, living creatures, archangels, and a host of other designations. They are created beings and are presently active in Heavenly locations. Since they are not believers in the sense I am explaining in this book, I left them out of the discussion earlier.

Another group that I have left out that occupies Heaven is the Old Testament Saints. These are men and women who lived by faith (and I would add with less information than you and I have). They trusted in what they had been told, believed that God had a solution for their sin, and waited for their Messiah. There is a long list of these folks, many who bear the familiar names of Moses, David, Abraham, Sarah and others. Since they are not believers in the same way as we in the Church Age are, I also separated them from our discussion.

There will also be other groups occupying Heaven. Typically called, 'Tribulational Saints," these people will live during the Tribulation period. They will have faith in Jesus Christ and gain salvation through His name. But they are to be considered distinct from the Church Age Believer in that they do not belong to the Body (or Bride) of Christ. In the chapters to follow, I will explain the events that transpire during the Tribulation period for the Church Age Believer. In essence, the Church Age Believer will be in Heaven receiving their rewards for service and participating in the Marriage of the Lamb while the

Tribulational Saints will be present on Earth. Since the Bride of Christ will be complete upon Christ's Second Coming, it is proper to separate the Church Age Believer from the Tribulational believer. I simply prefer to mark the Tribulational Saint as a distinct group as I do with the Old Testament Saint.

Along this same line, I would add another distinct group, the Millennial Saint. These folks will also be different than the Church Age Believer, yet because of their faith in Christ, they will occupy Heaven. However, for the focus in this book, I have also left them out of my discussion. It does not diminish them in any way, as it does not diminish the Trinity, God the Father, the Lord Jesus Christ, and the Holy Spirit, who are not mentioned in detail as occupants of Heaven even though they will be the central focus of it all. My purpose has only been to set our attention upon the one group, the Believer of this particular Church dispensation. I am aware that some would argue that the Tribulational Saint ought to be included in the Church dispensation. There has been a variety of presentations about dispensations and their duration. In this book, I determine that the Church dispensation begins on the Day of Pentecost (Acts 2) and concludes when the Bride of Christ is taken to Heaven at the time of the Rapture of the Church. Such a view does not omit the Tribulational Saint from Heaven in any way, but does show them to be distinct from the Body of Christ.

In this chapter, I want to set the focus again on the people in the present Church, Believers in Jesus Christ. The parameters of this group include every Believer from the birth of the Church (somewhere around AD 33, Acts 2) and extend to every Believer in the New Testament era following Acts 2. This would include people like Peter, Paul, Timothy, the apostles, the believers of the Thessalonian Church, the Ephesian Church, and the Philippian Church, to name a few. It would also include all the Believers in the 1st, 2nd, and 3rd centuries and counting up to the present century. Among these are Believers like William Tyndale, Martin Luther, John Calvin, Amy Carmichael and Fanny Crosby, and any throughout this world who have put their faith in Jesus Christ. What a list that makes! If the Lord continues to wait on His coming, there will be future Believers who will also put their faith in Him. I know that we like to think that we will be the last generation of the Church body, but God may have plans to add more generations to the Church.

All this to say, the parameters begin with the Church in Acts 2 and continue throughout history to this present age, and they will continue until Jesus Christ comes again for His Church, which is called the Rapture. This is the group I want to address in this chapter, because it has something to do with you and me, as well as God's plans in relation to Heaven.

The first thing to mention is our entrance into Heaven. As I have said before, there is no entrance into heaven apart from Jesus Christ. But, let's start with the assumption that you are a Believer. What is the next event on your timeline? You will be leaving this earth. It is quite possible that you will leave this earth by death. So far, only two people (Enoch and Elijah) have left this earth without dying in the Old Testament and no one in the New Testament has done it. Remember that even Jesus died before His resurrection and ascension. Should things continue as they are, God said it is appointed unto man once to die, and after that comes the judgment (Hebrews 9:27). Death is the penalty and consequence of sin. We are all sinners. Because we are descendants of Adam, we all have our part in physical death (Romans 5:12). Therefore, we expect that death is the typical event that will cause us to leave this earth.

Though this departure is the norm, we must include the fact that some Believers in the Church Age will leave the earth by means of the Rapture of the Church. This is the mystery that Paul wrote about in 1 Corinthians 15 and 1 Thessalonians 4. It will be the final departure for the Church Age Believer and will include all Believers in this dispensation. As it is described to us in these passages, no Church Believer will be left out. Those who are living at the time will be taken to Heaven and changed by the power of God. Those who have already died will find their physical bodies resurrected and they will be joined to them at that time. No matter what, whether one is alive or not at the Rapture of the Church, every Believer will be a participant in it. I will examine the details of this teaching in a few paragraphs. But this simple fact remains, we will leave this earth. That is the next event expected to happen.

Related to this, what happens if we depart before the Rapture? I believe there is evidence in the Bible that a Believer who dies, goes to Heaven to be in the presence of Jesus. They do not remain unconscious, nor does it seem that they are missing a body and existing as some sort of ghost. Consider the logic of 1 Thessalonians 4:13-14, "But we do not want you to be uninformed, brethren, about those who are asleep, so that you will not grieve as do the rest who have no hope. For if we believe that Jesus died and rose again, even so God will bring with Him those who have fallen asleep in Jesus." I emphasize the words of verse 14, *"even so God will bring with Him those who have fallen asleep in Jesus."* A few verses later, Paul writes, "Then we who are alive and remain will be caught up together with them in the clouds to meet the Lord in the air…" (v17). Notice the words, *"caught up together with them."* Who is this group that Paul has identified? They are the dead in Christ. The passage obviously states that they are with Him since they come with Him and the living Believer is caught up together with them. There is no other logical way to explain the passage. Some may question how they can be with Jesus and still be resurrected in verse 16 when the 'dead in Christ will rise first?' The answer to that question is not given in the Thessalonians passage, but is explained in 1 Corinthians 15:51-53. Their resurrection involves their physical bodies alone. As Paul states, we currently wear a perishable body. We have a mortal body. That means that we have bodies that are subject to perishing and dying. Vital to the passage is the fact that Paul teaches that a change must come about for our perishable, mortal bodies to be altered to fit a heavenly environment. At the Rapture of the Church the living bodies of the living Believers and the dead bodies of dead Believers will be changed from perishable to imperishable, mortal to immortal, and made capable of dwelling in a heavenly setting.

    The fact is that the body is not all there is to us. Adam was a body, fashioned by God out of the dust of the ground. But Adam was not alive until God breathed into him and man became a living soul. Even in the Old Testament, they understood that "the dust will return to the earth as it was, and the spirit will return to God who gave it" (Ecclesiastes 12:7). This is perfectly compatible with the New Testament teaching concerning the Believer who dies. Philippians 1:21-23 states, "For to me, to live is Christ and to die is gain. But if *I am* to live *on* in the flesh, this *will mean* fruitful labor for me; and I do not know which to choose. But I am hard-pressed from both *directions,* having the desire to depart and be with Christ, for *that* is very much better." Paul clearly states that when he departs he will be with Christ. That was not merely a wish, but a reality.

The same word construction can be found in 2 Corinthians 5:8, "we are of good courage, I say, and prefer rather to be absent from the body and to be at home with the Lord." It states that to be "with Christ" is to be "at home with the Lord." Neither verse suggests that to be absent from the body means that we will eventually be with the Lord. Rather, the events happen simultaneously. In other words, if you experience one, you also experience the other. There is nothing between the two phrases but the word "and."

Therefore when we put the pieces together we find that we will definitely be departing this earth, either by death or in the Rapture. Should we exit by death, we will go to be with Jesus in Heaven. When Jesus returns at the time of the Rapture, we would come with Him to meet the rest of the Church saints in the air. At that time, we will be joined again to our physical bodies that are changed from mortal to immortal. We do not know what kind of body we will wear between our death and the resurrection of our physical body. There are hints in the Bible that there is something that the present occupants of heaven wear. Some may think that they exist merely as spirits without bodies. However, there is something that makes up the shape and features of a body. They are certainly in a recognizable form. The disciples recognized Moses and Elijah at the transfiguration of Christ in Matthew 17:3. Even though Elijah did not die, but was translated to Heaven, we do have information that Moses did indeed die (Deuteronomy 34:5-6). Added to this is the very unusual verse in Jude 9 where Michael the archangel argued with Satan over the body of Moses. Though we may not understand the significance of the argument, at least it can be seen that Moses is still in a recognizable bodily form even though he does not possess his physical body. How Peter, James, and John realized that these two were Moses and Elijah is also beyond our understanding. Certainly they were not looking at spirits. If they had, would Peter have had the idea that they needed tents to dwell in while they were here?

Another consideration is from the story of Lazarus and the rich man. It is a story told by Jesus. He will never deceive us or merely fabricate a story. In the passage of Luke 16, we read the fact that the rich man (though he was not in heaven) still possessed eyes to lift up. He had a tongue that needed water. He was capable of talking. He experienced agony, thirst, and torment. On the other hand, Lazarus had a finger that the rich man suggested he dip in water so he could apply a drip to his thirsty tongue. Lazarus also was capable of being comforted. It is suggested that both of them possessed some sort of material body.

When the Rapture occurs, the physical bodies we currently wear will be changed. Should we have died prior to the Rapture, then we will be joined to our physical bodies and be like Jesus in a resurrected glorified body. Then, according to His promise, we will be with Him. Our activities will include participation with all the other saints in worshiping and serving our Savior, resting from our labors performed on earth, and anticipating the things He will do during the Rapture, Tribulation, Millennium and Eternal state. The events that follow the Rapture will require that we have a physical body. As Paul wrote in Philippians 3:21, Jesus will "transform the body of our humble state into conformity with the body of His glory, by the exertion of the power that He has even to subject all things to Himself." Then we will be ready to move on to the next phase of God's plan for the Believer.

CHAPTER 6
THE BELIEVER AND THE AWARDS IN HEAVEN

I believe that this chapter is a very important part of the whole teaching on the Believer and Heaven. As I seek to walk through the biblical evidences of what we can expect in the future, I am quite aware that we are entering into territory that some call controversial or even divisive. I recently received a flyer in the mail from a denomination that states that Heaven and Hell do not exist and they wanted to send me their teaching from the Bible to prove it. Honestly, they couldn't possibly deny the existence of Heaven using the Bible, unless they use a different interpretation of the word 'Heaven" or use a different method of interpretation for the whole Bible altogether. The reality is that sloppy hermeneutics produce sloppy theology. It is easy to come to wrong conclusions when one's approach to the Word is wrong.

It is my desire to follow a chronology for the Believer using a common sense and literal interpretation of Scripture. The Bible gives us many facts about Heaven and our relation to it, most of which are very easy to see and understand.

This chapter could easily be called "What the Believer will do during the Tribulation." Before I can explain what the Believer will be doing, there is a need to define the term "Tribulation." There are several opinions about what it is. Some do not believe that there will be an actual Tribulation. Some believe that it has happened already. Some believe that we are in the midst of it. And if that isn't enough, there are those who place the time of the Rapture before (Pre-tribulational Rapture), during (Mid-tribulational Rapture for one group and Pre-Wrath Rapture for another), and after (Post-tribulational Rapture) the Rapture. As I stated in the last chapter, the Pre-tribulational Rapture is supported by 1 Thessalonians 4, as well as several other related passages. The beginning place of this chapter concerns the fact of the Tribulation. Actually, it has nothing to do directly with the Believer, since there is Scriptural teaching that supports the wonderful truth that Believers will not be on the earth during this time. However, we tend to be incredibly curious about it. At best, we are similar to those who, when driving past an accident, slow down and strain to see as much as possible. I say this in regard to our future experience, but not in regard to our understanding. We must take notice of the teaching of the Bible concerning the Tribulation. It will be an incredible time of judgment on this earth. Seven years are foretold when God will pour out wrath upon this planet and upon those who reject His Word. Our knowledge of the reality of the Tribulation and its imminent arrival ought to propel us to be the greatest evangelists this world has seen. As Believers, we are not merely seeking an escape from our current world, but we should desire to have many go with us. Of the twenty two chapters in the book of Revelation, sixteen speak about the Tribulation. There are references in nearly all of the New Testament epistles to the Tribulation. Jesus spoke quite a bit about it, especially in Matthew 24 and 25. Most of the Old Testament prophets gave details about it as well. This chapter would be exceedingly lengthy if I were to examine all the passages that are given about the Tribulation and its description. Suffice it to say, that the presupposition for this chapter is that the Tribulation exists. It is yet in the future. It is after the Rapture. It does last seven years. And it is not based on some theological bias, but upon the ample testimony of God's Word. Since I am convinced from the Bible that the Believer does not have a part in the Tribulation as it takes place on earth, I merely state that the Believer will be active during the Tribulation, but that activity will take place in Heaven.

I believe that it is natural for those who plan a trip to a location they have never visited, to do their best to know about the place before they arrive. Thankfully, Heaven is not a mystery. We have a lot of information about it, but we must investigate carefully, putting each bit of evidence where it properly belongs. What we need to know about Heaven, God has told us. What He has not told us only leaves us to trust Him all the more.

To review the chronology given so far, the next event for the Believer will be to exit this earth and arrive in Heaven. If this exit is not by death, then it will certainly be in the Rapture. At the time of the Rapture, every Believer will be changed (1 Corinthians 15:52-53). The Believers who have died will be reunited with their resurrected bodies. The Believers who are alive will have their body changed from perishable and mortal to imperishable and immortal. According to 1 Corinthians 15:50 and 53, this is necessary because perishable and mortal bodies are not capable of dwelling in Heaven. We must be changed.

So, what are we to expect? The moment we leave this world, we go to be with the Lord (1 Thessalonians 4:17) and dwell with Him in Heaven in our glorified, resurrected, changed bodies. What a joy it will be to experience the reality of what John wrote, "we will be like Him, because we will see Him just as He is" (1 John 3:2). If you question whether this will happen, simply recall that the Lord "will transform the body of our humble state into conformity with the body of His glory, by the exertion of the power that He has even to subject all things to Himself" (Philippians 3:21). What a glorious anticipation! We shall be able to stand before the Lord "blameless" and "with great joy" (Jude 24). Literally, I can write for pages about the change the Lord will make in our bodies when He comes. But, this is not the end of the experience of Heaven. In fact, our future activities are just beginning when we arrive.

There are two main events that will transpire for the Believer while in Heaven. Both of these events are to take place during the time the earth is experiencing the Tribulation. How long each event takes place is not known, but there is evidence that both events will be complete at the end of the seven year Tribulation.

The first of these events is the Believer's judgment. I prefer to refer to it as the Believer's Award Ceremony. Two things are needed to be completed before this. First, the Believer must have completed all of his or her earthly ministry. Secondly, the entire Church must be present to be rewarded.

I am aware that there are some Believers who fear a judgment day. We have been taught the idea that our entire life will be projected on a screen for everyone to see – every good thing and every bad thing we have done – and that we will suffer intense humiliation. If that were true, I would be scared to death along with the rest. Who would look forward to such a thing?

I find it fascinating that the Apostle Paul was eager for this judgment. Perhaps you may think, "Of course Paul would be excited. He was some sort of 'super-Christian.'" Yet, he was the same man who wrote that he was the chief of sinners. I hardly think that he would be any different than you or me in the embarrassment of having our sins exposed. Rather, Paul writes that "in the day of Christ, I will have reason to glory" (Philippians 2:16), that 'he is able to guard what I have entrusted to Him until that day" (2 Timothy 1:12), and that "in the future there is laid up for me the crown of righteousness, which the Lord, the righteous Judge, will award to me on that day…" (2 Timothy 4:8). Here is a man who could not wait for judgment day. If only we were just as excited! We would be if we had the same ambition "to be pleasing to Him" (2 Corinthians 5:9). Why should we desire this? Because, as Paul writes in the same passage, "For we must all appear before the judgment seat of Christ, so that each one may be recompensed for his deeds in the body, according to what he has done, whether good or bad." Those last words get our attention. Let me explain them so that they will not be a distraction. First of all, the word "bad" is the Greek word that speaks of that which is worthless or of no account. It speaks of that which is good for nothing and is considered trivial. It does not refer to the concept of morals. There are other terms that express 'bad' or 'evil' as a moral and sinful thing. Those are not the terms used here. Remember that the issue of sin has been completely dealt with by the death of our Savior. He took our sins upon Himself and there is no condemnation to those who are in Christ Jesus (1 Peter 2:24; Romans 8:1). We take comfort in this truth while here on the earth. Our transport to Heaven will not change any part of it. It would be against His promise and His character to judge you for sins that He has already paid for at the cross. The Father will honor His Son's death. His sacrifice is sufficient for all of eternity, not just our few days on this earth. Therefore, whatever this judgment concerns in the term "bad" it cannot be sin related. Since we will be standing before the Lord in our glorified state, we will realize that we are not only saved from the penalty of sin, but also the presence of sin. So, this judgment is not to reveal sin. However, it does deal with the way we used our gifts and time. I picture our deeds (i.e., our service) being divided into two piles. One pile will consist of all deeds that were worthless. They have no value. If you have ever cleaned a garage, then you know what this pile looks like.

    Secondly, there is another pile that represents the good deeds. These, too, are the things that we will do through or by the body. "Good things" are contrasted with "worthless things." As explained in 1 Corinthians 3, only the good things will pass the test. At this point we should consider how it will be determined what things will be labeled "good." I believe the good things will be those which bring Christ glory. Not only will the deeds themselves be examined, but also the reason why we did them and how we did them. We must work for His glory, but also according to His strength. As He said, "Apart from Me, you can do nothing" (John 15:5). The things done in our own strength will count as worthless. Besides this, He knows our actions and our thoughts. Since His judgment is thorough, our attitudes will be considered. As a consequence, Paul stated, 'knowing the fear of the Lord, we persuade men, but we are made manifest to God..." (1 Corinthians 3:11).

As I wrote earlier, Paul longed for this judgment. That which will bring him joy is that which he will be recompensed for in his deeds. This phrase is not something negative. Rather, it is very encouraging. To recompense is to take care of something or provide for something. It corresponds with the words in Hebrews 6:10 "For God is not unjust so as to forget your work and the love which you have shown toward His name, in having ministered and in still ministering to the saints." The picture we are given is one that we see in athletic completion, especially at the Olympics. Those who perform well receive their award. In theological terms, we call the Believer's judgment 'The Bema Seat Judgment." It is a platform for awards. We have not seen the athletes punished in these ceremonies. In the same fashion, Paul stated that in that day, he will have reason to glory. He will receive the award.

It is my contention that this will be the first event the Believer will experience upon arrival in Heaven. It is proper for it to be a public ceremony, thus the whole Church must be present. All service on earth must be complete for the awards to be given. In keeping with the Heavenly scene, much praise will result from this grand evaluation. I only hope that I will make a contribution to the praise of that day.

A final consideration will lead us into the next chapter and the second event that must take place during those seven years. I believe this first event, the Believer's Award Ceremony, must take place to prepare us for the second event, the Marriage of the Lamb. The awards will be part of our wedding garment. More will be said about this in the chapter to follow, but as a simple thought, the Believer's judgment could hardly be a fearful thing in light of the preparation of the Bride for this glorious moment. Exciting things await us when we arrive in Heaven.

CHAPTER 7
THE BELIEVER AND THE MARRIAGE OF THE CHURCH IN HEAVEN

This chapter will involve the second great event in Heaven for the Believer. It is both mysterious and wonderful. Paul describes the relationship between Christ and the Church as a mystery (Ephesians 5:32). He also describes Christ's love for the Church (Ephesians 5:23-32), which is wonderful indeed. From the evidence of Scripture, the Believer will experience the Award Ceremony in Heaven during the seven year Tribulation period. They will also experience the Marriage of the Lord to the Church.

It is important to explain that the Bible uses the picture of marriage to express the unique relationship God has with His people. For example, it is stated in the Old Testament that God is married to Israel. In Isaiah 54:5 we read, "For your husband is your Maker, Whose name is the LORD of hosts; And your Redeemer is the Holy One of Israel, Who is called the God of all the earth." It is not the aim of this book to investigate Israel's relationship with God, but it is important that Israel and the Church be recognized as two separate identities. In the New Testament epistles, the teaching is that the Church is the Bride of Christ. Generally, those who seek to explain this relationship view the concept of the marriage as figurative concerning Christ and the Church. Yet, it is hard to get away from the way the marriage of the Lamb being described as an actual event. Key to understanding this are several passages I will explore in this chapter.

I have already shown that the judgment of the Believer (the Awards Ceremony) will take place in Heaven after the Rapture of the Church. Every Believer will be present and every deed of the Church will be completed. The Believers will receive rewards from the Lord for the works that have been done by His strength and wisdom, and according to His glory. At the completion of the ceremony, the Believer will be in possession of the awards (often referred to as 'crowns') given by the Lord. John exhorts his readers to abide in Christ, "so that when He appears, we may have confidence and not shrink away from Him in shame at His coming" (1 John 2:28). Though many may focus on the shrinking and shame that John mentions at the end of the verse, I think it important that the emphasis be given to abiding in Him and the confidence it will give to us on the day He appears. After all, the recompense will be a positive thing and is meant to show our Lord's appreciation for what we have done. In the end, it will be recognized that anything we have done was only accomplished because of Him. The idea that we will cast our crowns before His throne is taken from the actions of the twenty four elders in Revelation 4:9-11. After all, we served Him for His glory, not for ours. It would seem logical that we consider the rewards to be His and not ours. However, as explained in Ephesians 1:9-12, everything will be summed up to His glory – our works, our rewards, and even ourselves. Therefore, I certainly do not want to minimize the value of these rewards, as if they were disposable or were merely given as a small token of our Lord's appreciation which we would need to cast back before Him. We could ask the simple question, "If I am only going to enjoy the crowns or rewards for a few moments, then why did I work my whole life to earn them?" Perhaps this question could be answered in the following three purposes. First, I do believe the rewards will serve as acknowledgment from our Lord for what we have done in His name. Second, there is some recognition that these rewards actually belong to Him and that He will receive the ultimate glory for them. However, the third consideration is that He will receive the glory in the way He desires when He sees these rewards adorning the wedding garment of His Bride. From His perspective, the rewards serve a great purpose. When we consider all the grace He has showered upon us, all the power given that we may serve, and all the teaching of His word to bring us to maturity, we must realize that all of this is meant for more than just an Awards ceremony. I believe that He has been preparing us for the marriage ceremony.

The first passage to explore is Ephesians 5:22-32. Here Paul writes,

> Wives, *be subject* to your own husbands, as to the Lord. For the husband is the head of the wife, as Christ also is the head of the church, He Himself *being* the Savior of the body. But as the church is subject to Christ, so also the wives *ought to be* to their husbands in everything. Husbands, love your wives, just as Christ also loved the church and gave Himself up for her, so that He might sanctify her, having cleansed her by the washing of water with the word, that He might present to Himself the church

> in all her glory, having no spot or wrinkle or any such thing; but that she would be holy and blameless. So husbands ought also to love their own wives as their own bodies. He who loves his own wife loves himself; for no one ever hated his own flesh, but nourishes and cherishes it, just as Christ also *does* the church, because we are members of His body. FOR THIS REASON A MAN SHALL LEAVE HIS FATHER AND MOTHER AND SHALL BE JOINED TO HIS WIFE, AND THE TWO SHALL BECOME ONE FLESH. This mystery is great; but I am speaking with reference to Christ and the church.

Obviously, the teaching concerns the husband and his wife. Yet, in order to explain how the husband is to treat his wife, Paul uses the reality of Christ's love for the Church. That is the real standard by which we are to measure our human relationship. The facts are stated that Christ is the head of the Church and the Savior of the body. Christ loved the Church and gave Himself up for her. Christ sanctifies the Church and cleanses her by the washing with the Word. The church is nourished and cherished by Christ. All this so that Christ will present to Himself the Church in all her glory. Notice especially the event mentioned; He will present the Church to Himself. This presentation is in keeping with our Lord's prayer on behalf of the Church in John 17:22-26,

> The glory which You have given Me I have given to them, that they may be one, just as We are one; I in them and You in Me, that they may be perfected in unity, so that the world may know that You sent Me, and loved them, even as You have loved Me. Father, I desire that they also, whom You have given Me, be with Me where I am, so that they may see My glory which You have given Me, for You loved Me before the foundation of the world. O righteous Father, although the world has not known You, yet I have known You; and these have known that You sent Me; and I have made Your name known to them, and will make it known, so that the love with which You loved Me may be in them, and I in them.

What a beautiful picture of the Bride given to the Bridegroom and the Bridegroom giving to the Bride. They will share the glory. In a sense I picture a comical exchange. The Lord awards the Church for her service in His name. The Church casts it back because the glory belongs to Him. But, He wants the Church to wear it, so the awards are returned. So it seems that each one is trying to out-give the other, yet the Lord will have His way. Perhaps the best picture I can visualize is that the awards are placed on the Church, and since He insists that the Church wears them, the Church will ultimately just cast itself entirely before Him, rewards and all. Notice one more time that the Believer's judgment could not be about punishment. Who beats up his bride before the wedding? Rather, there the Church will stand as the Bride of Christ "in all her glory, having no spot or wrinkle or any such thing; but that she would be holy and blameless" (Ephesians 5:27). What a moment that will be! As Believers, we are the Church. We are the Bride of Christ.

How do I know that this event, the marriage of the Church to the Lord, will occur after the Rapture, after the judgment, and before the Second Coming of Christ to the earth? Why can it not take place much later? I believe the chronology given to us in the book of Revelation answers that question. By the time Revelation 19 takes place, the Rapture would have occurred and the Believers would be in Heaven. On earth there is a great Tribulation taking place for seven years. At the end of the Tribulation, Jesus comes down to the earth to finish the battle of Armageddon and to set up His millennial kingdom. Revelation 4-18 describes the Tribulation period. Revelation 19:1 begins with "after these things…" and then goes on to describe the Lord's coming in verse 11. What I find significant between these verses is the description of the Bride of Christ. Verses 7-9 states, "Let us rejoice and be glad and give the glory to Him, for the marriage of the Lamb has come and His bride has made herself ready." It was given to her to clothe herself in fine linen, bright *and* clean; for the fine linen is the righteous acts of the saints. Then he said to me, "Write, 'Blessed are those who are invited to the marriage supper of the Lamb.'" And he said to me, 'These are true words of God." The phrase, "for the marriage of the Lamb has come" is worded in a way that indicates that it is already finished. Also, the phrase, "it was given to her to clothe herself…" is already finished. Both phrases use the aorist verb in the Greek language –events that are complete. In contrast, those who are told these things are told to be rejoicing and to be glad now that these things have been done. It seems

51

right to call for praise in response to that which is seen or accomplished. Especially noteworthy is the fact that the clothing given to the Bride is 'the righteous acts of the saints.' Therefore, the Awards ceremony has been completed as well, before the wedding took place. After stating these things, a statement is made concerning those who are blessed to attend the marriage supper which follows.

As the chapter continues, Revelation 19:11-14 states:

> And I saw heaven opened, and behold, a white horse, and He who sat on it *is* called Faithful and True, and in righteousness He judges and wages war. His eyes *are* a flame of fire, and on His head *are* many diadems; and He has a name written *on Him* which no one knows except Himself. *He is* clothed with a robe dipped in blood, and His name is called The Word of God. And the armies which are in heaven, clothed in fine linen, white *and* clean, were following Him on white horses.

This is a description of the Lord's Second Coming. It is important to note that He does not come alone. There are other passages that speak of the fact that the Lord's angels will accompany Him at this return. But it is also true that the Bride will come with Him. Those who are described in these verses are clothed in the same way that the Bride is mentioned earlier. Also true to the fact is that the Lord has promised the Believer that wherever He is, we will be with Him. If the Lord is in Heaven, we will be with Him in Heaven. If the Lord returns to the earth, we shall return with Him. He intends to take His Bride with Him everywhere He goes. Remember what He said in John 14:3, "If I go and prepare a place for you, I will come again and receive you to Myself, that where I am, there you may be also." The same thing is stated in 1 Thessalonians 4:17, "Then we who are alive and remain will be caught up together with them in the clouds to meet the Lord in the air, and so we shall always be with the Lord." This describes the most beautiful marriage relationship of all – always and forever together.

This chapter was primarily focused on the second great event the Believer will experience in Heaven. Yet, there is much more said about the activities of Heaven during the Tribulation period. From the many chapters of the book of Revelation, we learn that while in Heaven, we will witness the worship of the angels and the living creatures. We will see the angels performing their duties in relation to the judgments on the earth. We will welcome new arrivals in Heaven – the martyred Tribulational saints. We will see an angelic conflict that will result in Satan's expulsion from Heaven. There is even a mention that all of Heaven will go quiet for a half hour in light of the judgments that are being poured out on the earth. Fascinating events are going to be witnessed firsthand by the Believer. Some people think that the Believer will be occupied watching the events that take place on the earth. Personally, I think that our time and focus will be occupied watching the things that take place on the throne. After all, we are told to "keep seeking the things above, where Christ is, seated at the right hand of God" and to set our minds on things above and not on the earth (Colossians 3:1-2). If that is our call while on this earth, how much more will it be when we reach Heaven? Certainly, it does reflect the focus of a Bride toward her Husband.

CHAPTER 8
THE BELIEVER AND THE SECOND COMING OF CHRIST

Myopia is a difficult disease to live with. I cannot remember a time in my life when I have not needed to wear glasses or contact lenses to correct my nearsightedness. Yet, I am thankful for the devices that are available to keep me from walking into walls. In a similar way, I am thankful for the Word of God that keeps us from 'spiritual myopia.' Far too often I see those who live with short-sightedness. Generally, the center of their focus is on themselves. I see it in individuals, but I also see it in the Church. Perhaps as pastors and teachers, we have contributed to this 'spiritual myopia' by stressing the Church so often, that we have lost focus of God's bigger plan. Granted, we do live in the Church Age. Our present ministries concern the Church. Even the focus of this book is the Church, the Believer and Heaven.

Some time ago I became aware that the Church is not the central focus of God's plan. Figuring from the view that the creation of the world was around 4000 BC and adding up the years that have focused on the Church since the Earth's creation, we estimate approximately 2000 years of history involving the Church to this present day. Already that discloses the estimate that 4000 years did not involve the Church. If we also suggest that the Rapture of the Church from this Earth takes place in this year, it would leave only 1007 remaining years of history (the seven year Tribulation and the 1000 year reign of Christ). Both of these events focus primarily upon Israel and her fulfilled prophecies as well as the unbeliever and the judgments upon this Earth. Neither of these directly involves the Church. Mathematically, the scenario I have just expressed involves the Church directly for 2000 of the 7007 years of history, not even 30 percent of it. This idea would certainly suggest that our focus on the Church, as if it were the centerpiece of all history, is somewhat nearsighted. This may be quite the comment in light of the last chapter and the wonderful description of the Church in all her beauty before the throne of God. However, it is at this point that we must realize that time has not ended simply because the Church has arrived in Heaven and has taken its place alongside the Lord. There is much more for us to see. The following chapters will help us to see the magnificent perspective of God's plan, and how the Believer is involved in it.

Realize for a few moments how precious it is to have the Bible's explanation of time and events. If we were to stand in Adam's sandals and look into the future, generally our view would involve two things. The first would be that we will die. The second that God has promised in the seed of Adam, One who would bruise the serpent's head (Genesis 3:15).

If we were to see from Enoch's view, we would add a promise that the Lord will come in judgment upon the ungodly at His second coming (Jude 1:14-15). However, Enoch certainly would not have considered this a second coming. The program of the Lord's comings to Earth had not been revealed at that point. Neither Adam nor Enoch's future view included things outside of events upon this Earth.

Job's perspective included more than just death and the promise of the Lord's coming to deal with sinners. He stated his confidence that "even after my skin is destroyed, yet from my flesh I shall see God" (Job 19:26). Suddenly, our view from his standpoint has gone beyond merely an earthly existence, yet it is so limited.

Along came Abraham and sight starts to expand. Abraham knew all too well the story of death. Yet he also had a perspective beyond this world in that "he was looking for the city which has foundations, whose architect and builder is God" (Hebrews 11:10). Faith opened his eyes to wondrous things that the Lord had in store for those who trusted Him. Little by little, the Lord revealed His plan to the prophets of the Old Testament era. The fact of man's departure by death was strongly reinforced through repetition. However, the promise of the Redeemer and His sacrifice on man's behalf, as well as His judgments upon the ungodly, became more and more evident.

If we were to stand in the prophet's sandals, our view would include some details of the Tribulation (as Daniel and so many others gave); the coming of the Lord (though it was hard to understand the distinction between the first and second coming); the kingdom of the Messiah; and Isaiah's explanation of the destruction of the old Earth and Heaven and the creation of a new Earth and Heaven. Even the first 30 years of the Gospel era had the same focal point. Is it any wonder that the information about the Church, the Rapture, the Believer's judgment and the Bride of Christ is explained as a mystery by Paul? What a privilege we have to see so much in contrast to those who lived and saw so little. That the Lord has given us this view is humbling. Yet, it also holds us accountable to what we know. He has not revealed these things so that we may develop an attitude of self-importance, but that we may bring Him the glory He rightly deserves. Throughout our stay in Heaven, our frequent activity will involve the worship of Christ. We will be observers of some of the most magnificent and the most terrible events in all of history, and yet our focus will be on Him.

It is my opinion and speculation that while we are occupying Heaven, our desire will not be to watch the events that take place upon Earth. It just seems to me that it would be odd for us, who are told to 'fix our eyes on Jesus' and to keep seeking things above, to arrive in Heaven only to set our eyes on things below. There will be plenty in Heaven to hold our attention. The Book of Revelation tells us much about what events we will be seeing while there. As the Tribulation begins on Earth, Revelation 4 and 5 speaks of a worship service in Heaven. The Church will be present and will have its focus riveted to the Throne of Christ. We will witness our Lord breaking the seals that initiate the judgments upon the Earth (Revelation 6). As the wrath is being poured out, we will begin to see new arrivals in Heaven – the martyred Tribulational Saints (Revelation 6:9-11; 7:9-17). We will hear conversations in Heaven and see the activities of the angels in administering the judgments from the Lord. We will experience an amazing moment when the seventh seal judgment is opened. There will be the unique half hour of silence in Heaven. I cannot fathom the nature of that event – yet we will be there to witness it (Revelation 8:1). How fascinating it will be in contrast to the constant sound we will hear of the seraphim circling the throne of God while calling out "Holy, Holy, Holy, is the Lord of Earth" (Isaiah 6:3). The effects of silence will truly be awesome.

Revelation chapters 8 through 11 unfold a series of judgments, each one intensifying the Lord's wrath upon the ungodly of this Earth. Yet, these events are not all that will take place. While we watch, it appears that Satan's banishment from Heaven will take place before us. Scholars have wrestled with Revelation 12:7-12 and have come to differing opinions as to when it takes place. From the context of Revelation 12, it seems to best fit during the Tribulation. The pronouns and descriptions of those rejoicing in verses 10 and 11 answer best to the

Tribulational Saints. According to verse 12, the persecution of these saints is intensified after Satan has been thrown down. All of this would suggest that we will be witnesses of the battle between Michael and his angels with Satan and his demons and the outcome leading to Satan's expulsion from Heaven during the Tribulational period. I have heard some even suggest that the very reason the first Heaven will be destroyed is because Satan's footprints have been in it. At least we know that our accuser has been very active in that role before the throne of God.

At this point you may be noticing that our experiences in Heaven are not those of a hammock, a harp, sunshine, lemonade and a fluffy cloud to rest upon. Rather, we will be in the presence of the Sovereign God and with our Savior, Jesus Christ. There, we shall see and hear the things that relate to the presentation of the bowl judgments (Revelation 15) and the song of the 144,000 elect Jews (Revelation 14). Seven years of judgment will approach its climax as we watch the activities that surround the throne. The moment of the Lord's departure to the Earth in His second coming will arrive. Is it any wonder that this great event will be preceded by a worship service in Heaven? Revelation 19 begins:

> After these things I heard something like a loud voice of a great multitude in heaven, saying, "Hallelujah! Salvation and glory and power belong to our God; BECAUSE HIS JUDGMENTS ARE TRUE AND RIGHTEOUS; for He has judged the great harlot who was corrupting the earth with her immorality, and HE HAS AVENGED THE BLOOD OF HIS BOND-SERVANTS ON HER." And a second time they said, "Hallelujah! HER SMOKE RISES UP FOREVER AND EVER." And the twenty-four elders and the four living creatures fell down and worshiped God who sits on the throne saying, "Amen. Hallelujah!" And a voice came from the throne, saying, "Give praise to our God, all you His bond-servants, you who fear Him, the small and the great." Then I heard *something* like the voice of a great multitude and like the sound of many waters and like the sound of mighty peals of thunder, saying, "Hallelujah! For the Lord our God, the Almighty, reigns" (Revelation 19:1-6).

What a moment this will be! The judgments of the Tribulation will be at an end. The Battle of Armageddon is prepared to take place. The kings of the earth have raised their fist to Heaven and have refused to acknowledge the authority of God.

We, the Church, will also have been prepared for this moment. Our rewards will have been given and the marriage will have taken place (Revelation 19:7-8). Now we are seen as more than just the Bride of Christ. We are described as an army (Revelation 19:14). Our Lord will take His place to descend to the Earth:

> And I saw heaven opened, and behold, a white horse, and He who sat on it *is* called Faithful and True, and in righteousness He judges and wages war. His eyes *are* a flame of fire, and on His head *are* many diadems; and He has a name written *on Him* which no one knows except Himself. *He is* clothed with a robe dipped in blood, and His name is called The Word of God (Revelation 19:11-13).

As He leaves Heaven, we shall go with Him according to the promise that we will be with Him forever. "And the armies which are in heaven, clothed in fine linen, white *and* clean, were following Him on white horses" (Revelation 19:14). Some commentators believe that this army is angelic. I do not doubt that angels will accompany Him at His return. Matthew 25:31 states, "But when the Son of Man comes in His glory, and all the angels with Him, then He will sit on His glorious throne." However, I am convinced that the promise "so shall we always be with the Lord" (1 Thess. 4:17) puts us present at His coming too. After all, why would He leave His Bride in Heaven as He begins His reign for 1000 years on Earth?

This may come as a surprise to the reader, but I believe that when we leave the first Heaven, we will not return to it again. Its purpose concerning us will be over. This is in keeping with God's plan to create a New Heaven and a New Earth after the 1000 year reign of Christ. This is also in keeping with the concept that the 'dwelling places' of John 14:2 ("In My Father's house are many dwelling places...") are temporary resting places and not permanent 'mansions.'

As we descend with Jesus Christ at His Second Coming, it seems that we shall come to the battle as spectators rather than as participants. Only Christ is seen with a sword (Revelation 19:15). The Church (i.e., the army) does not have any weapon at all (Revelation 19:14). We shall simply be 'with Him,' as Revelation 17:14 states, "These will wage war against the Lamb, and the Lamb will overcome them, because He is Lord of lords and King of kings, and those who are with Him *are the* called and chosen and faithful." Our coming with Him will be for the purpose of reigning with Him:

> He who overcomes, and he who keeps My deeds until the end, TO HIM I WILL GIVE AUTHORITY OVER THE NATIONS; AND HE SHALL RULE THEM WITH A ROD OF IRON, AS THE VESSELS OF THE POTTER ARE BROKEN TO PIECES, as I also have received *authority* from My Father (Revelation 2:26-27, see also Revelation 19:15).

What a glorious moment it will be. How refreshing to read once again, "Therefore, my beloved brethren, be steadfast, immovable, always abounding in the work of the Lord, knowing that your toil is not *in* vain in the Lord" (1 Corinthians 15:58).

Now that I have us on the descent to the Earth, it is proper that I complete the episode for you that you may see what is all to occur at the second coming of Christ. Three significant events are part of this return and we will witness each one.

The first, and perhaps the most well-known event, will be the war involving Christ and the armies of the world. There is a section of Zechariah, chapters 12 through 14, that records this war in graphic precision. The descriptions are so vivid that it is tempting to call Zechariah the "Old Testament Book of Revelation." Even as we are prone to go to the Book of Daniel for our studies of eschatology, the comparison makes Daniel's prophecies appear black and white, and Zechariah's appear full color. I will give a summary of the battle log here and leave the joy of reading the passage to you.

What we find just prior to the Lord's second coming are the armies of the world gathered in a valley just north and west of Jerusalem. All other cities appear to be captured or surrounded, and the remnant of the Jews are held siege in the city of Jerusalem. The nations surrounding them are confident that their long awaited plan of eliminating the Jews from the face of the earth is about to be realized.

These armies are led by the Antichrist and he is empowered by Satan himself. Sometime during these events, the focus will shift from the Jews to an actual threat against the Lord God. Blood thirsty leaders are never satisfied, even in victory. They desire another conquest. Satan is behind the activity, and his goal and passion is still to overthrow the Lord and claim His throne. As a result the Antichrist will in a sense raise his fist toward Heaven and taunt the Lord, saying something like, "Now, this is an army that you cannot defeat!"

What is surprising to some is that the Antichrist will be victorious over the city of Jerusalem. It will be obvious to the Jews within the city that they will soon be captured. A portion of them will escape toward the city of Petra, a distance of nearly 100 miles south of Jerusalem in the territory we call Edom or Bozrah.

Zechariah describes a fierce war between the Jews and the armies of the Antichrist. For a while, the Jews will have the upper hand and will defend their city. There are indications that the Jews will be victorious after all. However, as Zechariah 14:1-2 states:

> Behold, a day is coming for the LORD when the spoil taken from you will be divided among you. For I will gather all the nations against Jerusalem to battle, and the city will be captured, the houses plundered, the women ravished and half of the city exiled, but the rest of the people will not be cut off from the city.

The city will fall. Its occupants will be killed or captured. Plans will be made to exterminate them, but the realization that some have escaped to the area of Petra has transfixed the Antichrist's attention. He will not be content with destroying only part of them. So he will hold his captives in the city, and he will turn his armies toward Bozrah to grasp the rest of them.

As the armies approach, the Jews in that area are completely trapped. Humanly speaking, the Antichrist senses that he has finally won and the Jews sense that they are finally doomed. But, according to Zechariah 12, something spiritual and wonderful begins. The Lord will pour out the Holy Spirit upon these Jews and they will realize for the first time that Jesus Christ is the Savior. They will mourn for their sins for two days and then suddenly will cry out for the first time since Jesus went into the city of Jerusalem over 2,000 years ago, "Blessed is He who comes in the Name of the Lord" (Matthew 23:39). Zechariah declares, "Then the LORD will go forth and fight against those nations, as when He fights on a day of battle" (Zechariah 14:3).

Now we perk up our attention, for this is that part that includes the Believer. As stated in Revelation 19:11, the Lord and His armies descend from Heaven. His first matter of business seems to be at Bozrah. Isaiah 34:6 states, "The sword of the LORD is filled with blood, It is sated with fat, with the blood of lambs and goats, With the fat of the kidneys of rams. For the LORD has a sacrifice in Bozrah And a great slaughter in the land of Edom." Habakkuk 3:3 adds, "God comes from Teman, And the Holy One from Mount Paran. Selah. His splendor covers the heavens, And the earth is full of His praise." Teman and Mount Paran are in the vicinity of Bozrah. This may be a bit surprising to you that His first stop will be in this territory, especially since we have been taught for years that Jesus' arrival would be on the Mount of Olives. We remember the words that the angels told the disciples when Jesus ascended into heaven: "Men of Galilee, why do you stand looking into the sky? This Jesus, who has been taken up from you into heaven, will come in just the same way as you have watched Him go into heaven" (Acts 1:11). I think a close look at this passage does not state that this will be the first location of His arrival, but it mentions the manner of His arrival.

Isaiah 63:3-6 describes the Lord's attack:

> I have trodden the wine trough alone, And from the peoples there was no man with Me. I also trod them in My anger And trampled them in My wrath; And their lifeblood is sprinkled on My garments, And I stained all My raiment. For the day of vengeance was in My heart, And My year of redemption has come. I looked, and there was no one to help, And I was astonished and there was no one to uphold; So My own arm brought salvation to Me, And My wrath upheld Me. I trod down the peoples in My anger And

made them drunk in My wrath, And I poured out their lifeblood on the earth.

No doubt you have noticed the statements "no one to help" and have thought, "But, is not the Lord's army with Him?" I cannot say dogmatically, but I think the Lord is referring to the Jews in that they are incapable of doing anything at this point. This reminds me of Peter, who was willing to defend the Lord at His arrest, but proved to be unable to be of any help at all. Yet, the description of this battle by Isaiah is the answer to the questions, "Why is Your apparel red, And Your garments like the one who treads in the wine press?" (Isaiah 63:2) and "Who is this who comes from Edom, With garments of glowing colors from Bozrah, This One who is majestic in His apparel, Marching in the greatness of His strength? It is I who speak in righteousness, mighty to save" (Isaiah 63:1).

The battle sounds so fierce, but remember that it is in response to the desperate plea of His own people. Micah records:

> I will surely assemble all of you, Jacob, I will surely gather the remnant of Israel. I will put them together like sheep in the fold; Like a flock in the midst of its pasture They will be noisy with men. The breaker goes up before them; They break out, pass through the gate and go out by it. So their king goes on before them, And the LORD at their head (Micah 2:12-13).

What a pleasant picture! One moment it appeared that they were finished and the next they are walking behind their conquering Captain.

However, the battle is not yet over. There are still Jews being held in Jerusalem. Apparently the Antichrist falls back to claim them since there was no success at Bozrah. Yet, their retreat will not succeed. The Scriptures state that the blood will rise to the bridle of a horse in depth and its length will be nearly 200 miles in distance (Revelation 14:19-20). As it says in Revelation 19:15-19,

> From His mouth comes a sharp sword, so that with it He may strike down the nations, and He will rule them with a rod of iron; and He treads the wine press of the fierce wrath of God, the

Almighty. And on His robe and on His thigh He has a name written, "KING OF KINGS, AND LORD OF LORDS." Then I saw an angel standing in the sun, and he cried out with a loud voice, saying to all the birds which fly in midheaven, 'Come, assemble for the great supper of God, so that you may eat the flesh of kings and the flesh of commanders and the flesh of mighty men and the flesh of horses and of those who sit on them and the flesh of all men, both free men and slaves, and small and great." And I saw the beast and the kings of the earth and their armies assembled to make war against Him who sat on the horse and against His army.

The final stage of the battle will be in Jerusalem. Then, as Zechariah explains:

In that day His feet will stand on the Mount of Olives, which is in front of Jerusalem on the east; and the Mount of Olives will be split in its middle from east to west by a very large valley, so that half of the mountain will move toward the north and the other half toward the south. You will flee by the valley of My mountains, for the valley of the mountains will reach to Azel; yes, you will flee just as you fled before the earthquake in the days of Uzziah king of Judah. Then the LORD, my God, will come, *and all the holy ones with Him!* (Zechariah 14:4-5).

Believer, you will see this day for you will be with the Lord at His coming.

There is a second part to this great war. It includes the defeat of the Antichrist and the False Prophet. The book of Revelation helps us again:

And I saw the beast and the kings of the earth and their armies assembled to make war against Him who sat on the horse and against His army. And the beast was seized, and with him the false prophet who performed the signs in his presence, by which he deceived those who had received the mark of the beast and those who worshiped his image; these two were thrown alive into the lake of fire which burns with brimstone. And the rest were killed with the sword which came from the mouth of Him who sat on the horse, and all the birds were filled with their flesh (Revelation 19:19-21).

Judgment of beast & false prophet...

As far as I can tell, these will be the only two who will never stand before the Lord on the day of judgment. Their judgment is complete and they are sealed forever in the Lake of Fire. A related passage is found in Isaiah 14:16-21. Some attribute the passage to Satan, but the similarities to the Antichrist – who seems to operate as Satan incarnated – leaves a possibility that it is he who is being described.

> "Those who see you will gaze at you, They will ponder over you, *saying,* 'Is this the man who made the earth tremble, Who shook kingdoms, Who made the world like a wilderness And overthrew its cities, Who did not allow his prisoners to *go* home?' "All the kings of the nations lie in glory, Each in his own tomb. "But you have been cast out of your tomb Like a rejected branch, Clothed with the slain who are pierced with a sword, Who go down to the stones of the pit Like a trampled corpse. "You will not be united with them in burial, Because you have ruined your country, You have slain your people. May the offspring of evildoers not be mentioned forever. "Prepare for his sons a place of slaughter Because of the iniquity of their fathers. They must not arise and take possession of the earth And fill the face of the world with cities."

Apparently, his entire household will be killed for fear that they will become like him. I realize that much is said and feared about the Antichrist. Surely the world has yet to see a tyrant like him. But, make this certain in your thinking, it is the Lord who is the King of kings and the Lord of lords. There is no one higher than He is. When we see this day, a mighty hallelujah will rise up from the saints of the Lord.

One more aspect of the war must be fulfilled, and the Lord will have complete victory. It involves the biggest enemy we have. Revelation 20:1-2 states, 'Then I saw an angel coming down from heaven, holding the key of the abyss and a great chain in his hand. And he laid hold of the dragon, the serpent of old, who is the devil and Satan, and bound him for a thousand years." This will not be the final event concerning him. However, in light of the kingdom the Lord is establishing on the Earth at this time, Satan must be bound for its duration. More will be said about him in the chapters to come.

I doubt that I have exhausted the topic of the Lord's return, but these things are sufficient to show us that being with the Lord will be far from boring. How often I have heard, "Just what will we be doing up there?" The answer is clearly that much will be done "up there" and "down here" too. Remember, wherever our Lord goes, so does the Believer.

CHAPTER 9
THE BELIEVER AND THE MILLENNIAL KINGDOM/ REIGN OF CHRIST

A little while ago I had the privilege of listening to a series of lectures on the book of Revelation by Dr. Charles Ryrie. As he came to the twentieth chapter, he announced that we were going to have a quiz concerning the Millennium. His first question asked us to spell the word 'Millennium.' We all chuckled at the fact that it proved to be far more difficult for some of us than we thought it would be. He went on to make the point that the Millennium, for some, is even harder to understand than to spell the word. I know it is true, but I am also saddened by the fact. The Bible says a great deal about the Millennium. In fact, there is more information about the Millennium in the Old Testament than in the New Testament. Its importance has not diminished in the New Testament, even though the word "Millennium" is not found in the Scriptures. "Millennium" is a Latin term that combines the term "year" (*annus*) with the term "thousand" (*mille*) and speaks of a 1000 year duration of time. In three verses in Revelation 20 (verses 4, 5 & 6) John speaks of a duration of 1000 years in which Christ will reign and others will come to life and reign with Him. As straightforward as the statements are in the verses, it seems incredible that there are critics who claim that there is no Millennium or that it ought to be seen as allegorical or figurative. Others believe that we are in the Millennium at this moment or that it is taking place in Heaven as Christ sits on the throne of David. Still others emphasize that the Millennium is the time in which the Church will gain the promises that Israel lost due to their disobedience. Is it any wonder that the Church is confused and chooses to dismiss the topic? I prefer to let the Scriptures state what it does in a literal way. Revelation 20 teaches that there will be a 1000 year reign of Jesus Christ from Jerusalem over the whole earth. It also teaches that He does not reign alone.

> Then I saw thrones, and they sat on them, and judgment was given to them. And I *saw* the souls of those who had been beheaded because of their testimony of Jesus and because of the word of God, and those who had not worshiped the beast or his

image, and had not received the mark on their forehead and on their hand; and they came to life and reigned with Christ for a thousand years (Revelation 20:4). The rest of the dead did not come to life until the thousand years were completed. This is the first resurrection (Revelation 20:5). Blessed and holy is the one who has a part in the first resurrection; over these the second death has no power, but they will be priests of God and of Christ and will reign with Him for a thousand years (Revelation 20:6).

In those three verses there are six direct statements about a thousand years.'

As has been my desire throughout this book, I will seek to show the relationship of the Believer to this next great event on the Lord's prophetic calendar. The reality is that the Believer does have a part in the Millennial Reign of Christ. This fact I have explained previously. Jesus has promised the Believer that when we go to be with Him, we will also go with Him wherever He is. When He is in Heaven, the Believer will be in Heaven with Him. When He comes again to the earth at the time of the Battle of Armageddon, the Believer will come with Him. When He sets up His kingdom and reigns in Jerusalem for 1000 years, the Believer will be with Him. As Paul said, "….and so shall we always be with the Lord" (1 Thessalonians 4:17).

The question that we may have at this point is, "What will Believers be doing in the Millennial Kingdom?" In order to answer this, I will first explain the purpose and the promise of the Millennial Period. The majority of the information Scripture gives to us involves Israel and the Millennial Kingdom. It is important that we sift through it carefully.

First of all, the Lord has made a promise to Abraham and his descendants concerning the land which He gave to him. In Genesis 15:18 it states, 'On that day the LORD made a covenant with Abram, saying, 'To your descendants I have given this land, From the river of Egypt as far as the great river, the river Euphrates.'' It is noteworthy that this full piece of land has not been secured, even in the days of Solomon. That promise has yet to be fulfilled. God will bring the realization of it about during the Millennium when Abraham and his descendants will enjoy the fullness of the promise.

Second of all, the Lord has made a promise to David concerning his throne and a particular Descendant who will be able to reign on that throne forever. The promise is made in 2 Samuel 7 and explained in Isaiah 9:6-7,

> For a child will be born to us, a son will be given to us; And the government will rest on His shoulders; And His name will be called Wonderful Counselor, Mighty God, Eternal Father, Prince of Peace. There will be no end to the increase of *His* government or of peace, on the throne of David and over his kingdom, to establish it and to uphold it with justice and righteousness From then on and forevermore. The zeal of the LORD of hosts will accomplish this.

An important aspect of this promise is that it demands a king capable of living forever to fulfill the prophecy. That promise has yet to be fulfilled. God will bring the realization of it about during the Millennium and David and his descendants will enjoy the fullness of the promise when Jesus reigns on the throne.

So far, I have explained two promises that will require the Millennium for their fulfillment, but neither of these promises relate directly to the Church or the Believer. They are promises to the people of Israel. The same is true of another promise to Daniel the prophet. "But as for you, go *your way* to the end; then you will enter into rest and rise *again* for your allotted portion at the end of the age" (Daniel 12:13). What is true of Daniel is also true of Abraham, David, and the other Old Testament saints. They have lived their lives and died. But they will also rise again and receive their allotted portions at the end of the age. If the promise was made to them about the Millennial kingdom, doesn't it make sense that they will be resurrected to fulfill it? The need for the millennial kingdom to exist is to fulfill the promises that the Lord made over and over to His people, the Jews, concerning the land, the throne, and their enjoyment of it all.

Added to these basic facts is the Bible's description of the changes to the earth, especially around the city of Jerusalem. Mountains will be knocked down and the city itself will be raised higher than all others. A river will flow from the city and make the waters of the Dead

Sea fresh and teeming with fish. A new temple will be constructed and the nations of the earth will be required to come each year for the Feast of Tabernacles to worship the Lord in Jerusalem. Best of all, Jesus will reign in righteousness and with a rod of iron. It will be the first time ever that this world will know what it is to have a spiritually centered government in the fullest measure. Imagine, a government that is completely righteous in all its dealings and an unsurpassed time of peace with the Prince of Peace reigning. Agriculture will be released from its curse, even to the place where deserts will produce a harvest. People will be eager to learn of the Lord and will worship together. With all these great things occurring, it is remarkable that the sin of mankind will continue to ruin that which is good. A rebellion of mankind, a group described in number as the 'sands of the sea,' will take their stand against the Lord in His reign (Revelation 20:8). These promises have yet to be fulfilled. God will bring the realization of them about during the Millennium and Abraham and his descendants will enjoy the fullness of the promises.

There are other promises that must be fulfilled during the Millennium that do not relate to the Church. For example, there will be unique rulers in the Millennium. Several prophecies in Jeremiah (30:9) and Ezekiel (37:24-25) speak directly to David himself ruling over the Israelites, somewhat like a governor ruling under the authority of a king:

> My servant David will be king over them, and they will all have one shepherd; and they will walk in My ordinances and keep My statutes and observe them. They will live on the land that I gave to Jacob My servant, in which your fathers lived; and they will live on it, they, and their sons and their sons' sons, forever; and David My servant will be their prince forever (Ezekiel 37:24-25).

Obviously, David would need to be resurrected for this to be fulfilled. This is another proof that the Old Testament saints will be enjoying the literal promises of the Lord.

Another group that will have a special designation in the Millennial Kingdom is the apostles who were with Christ when He was on the Earth. Jesus promised them, "Truly I say to you, that you who have followed Me, in the regeneration when the Son of Man will sit on

His glorious throne, you also shall sit upon twelve thrones, judging the twelve tribes of Israel" (Matthew 19:28). Again, a resurrection must take place prior to the Millennium for these to reign with Christ. How unique this will be!

Consider what changes would need to take place in the world's data-base for census figures. The population of the world will include resurrected Old Testament saints in glorified bodies and apparently without physical limitations. Logically, they will not be subject to the decay of age or death. Among them will be the Church Age Believers in 'post-rapture' glorified bodies, also not subject to the decay of age or death. At this point, the Tribulational saints can be added to the roster of those who have been resurrected.

> And I *saw* the souls of those who had been beheaded because of their testimony of Jesus and because of the word of God, and those who had not worshiped the beast or his image, and had not received the mark on their forehead and on their hand; and they came to life and reigned with Christ for a thousand years (Revelation 20:4).

Besides the resurrected saints, there will also be living saints who survived the Tribulation and have entered into the Kingdom of Christ. I believe that many of the parables found in Matthew 24 and 25 speak about these who the Lord will bring out of the Tribulation to enjoy the Millennium. However, these will still be in the normal human state that we know too well. They will be subject to the decay of age and death. They will also be capable of sinning. But, from what can be gathered from Scripture, they will be capable of living enormous periods of time much like the people who lived before the flood. From these, there will be others who are born and the world will be populated and nations will exist. Jesus Christ will rule over these nations for the duration of 1000 years.

Much can be said about the characteristics of this period, but I will attempt to keep my focus in this study. The primary question of this chapter has to do with the relationship of the Believer and the Millennial Kingdom. What will we be doing during this time?

As I have stated before, the Church will definitely be present on the earth at the time of the Millennial Kingdom. It is the fulfillment of the promise that we will always be with the Lord. But, it must be stated that the Church will not be here to take the place of Israel or to receive any of the promises that the Lord directly made to Israel or its people. A distinction must be made between the Church and Israel and the Bible states it clearly.

The role of the Church in the Millennium is spelled out in Revelation 20:4 and 20:6. As John records what he saw, he writes, "Then I saw thrones, and they sat on them." Who are "they?" They cannot be the Tribulational saints because they are mentioned separately in the same verse, which implies that they will reign as well. Backing up in the text, we know that John is not talking about Satan, since he will be locked up for the 1000 years (Revelation 20:1-3) or the beast and false prophet (they were thrown into the Lake of Fire in 19:20). It wouldn't be logical for these three to reign with Christ anyway. We can certainly eliminate the armies of the Earth that Jesus destroys upon His arrival (Revelation 19:15). The next group encountered in this backward approach is found in Revelation 19:14 "And the armies which are in heaven, clothed in fine linen, white *and* clean, were following Him on white horses." These are the Believers who are the Bride of Christ. Since the Bride will be with Christ and will also reign with Him, it makes sense that these thrones will be occupied by the Church. Added to this, verse 6 states that "they will be priests of God and of Christ and will reign with Him for a thousand years" (Revelation 20:6). The description matches that of the Believer since the second death will have no power over them (verse 6).

What will be the duty of the Church during the Millennial reign? It would be in relation to the fact that "they will be priests" (verse 6). While the role of a prophet was to represent God to man, the role of a priest was to represent man to God. A similar concept is seen in the Old Testament priest and his role in leading the people in worship to God. Peter writes that the Church is "A CHOSEN RACE, A royal PRIESTHOOD, A HOLY NATION, A PEOPLE FOR *God's* OWN POSSESSION, so that you may proclaim the excellencies of Him who has called you out of darkness into His marvelous light" (1 Peter 2:9). This is echoed by the elders before the throne in Revelation 5:9-10,

> And they sang a new song, saying, 'Worthy are You to take the book and to break its seals; for You were slain, and purchased for God with Your blood *men* from every tribe and tongue and people and nation. You have made them *to be* a kingdom and priests to our God; and they will reign upon the earth.'

Chronologically, this reference is made before the Tribulation begins in Revelation 6. Therefore, I do not believe it is a direct reference to the Tribulational saints and it cannot be a reference to the Old Testament saints either, since it highlights the purchase of Christ with His blood and those who are saved because of it. Significant to this passage is that those who are purchased are made a 'kingdom' and 'priests' and they will reign upon the earth.' The information is compatible with the Church, especially in its role as 'priests.' It would seem fitting that the Church is well suited for this purpose in the Millennial period. The world of mankind will be led to worship Christ through the testimony and ministry of the Church. Honestly, who would be better at this than those who know Him so well? After all, the Church is the Bride of Christ and according to Ephesians 1:12, our existence has a purpose, 'to the end that we who were the first to hope in Christ would be to the praise of His glory." That will be our permanent occupation. Shall we expect it to be suspended during the Millennial Age? The reality is that if we are not praising the Lord and leading others to worship Him now, we are not practicing what we are called to do forever. As priests to Christ, that is our role, especially in the Millennial Kingdom.

In addition to the role of priest, the Church will be given the role of judging the world and the angels. This is an interesting aspect that comes with very little information to explain. What is clear is that Paul reprimanded the Corinthian Believers with the comment:

> Does any one of you, when he has a case against his neighbor, dare to go to law before the unrighteous and not before the saints? Or do you not know that the saints will judge the world? If the world is judged by you, are you not competent *to constitute* the smallest law courts? Do you not know that we will judge angels? How much more matters of this life? (1 Corinthians 6:1-3).

The concept of the Greek word *krinō* includes both the ability to judge and the ability to rule or govern. Some suggest that the Church will be given judgment over the world and over fallen angels. I am not so sure that any judgment related to sin is suggested, since it is the primary task of the Lord to judge sin and the sinful world and fallen angels are already under His judgment (2 Peter 2:4; Jude 6). It seems more likely that the Believer will have a role in governing the world and the good angels. After all, the angels are "ministering spirits" who serve the saints (Hebrews 1:14). As the Bride of Christ, it seems logical that angels will continue to serve the Church throughout eternity, even though the nature of that service is unknown. The information is sufficient for me to come to the conclusion that the Church will have the responsibility of ruling in the Millennial Period.

I doubt that I have scratched the surface of this aspect of the Believer and the Millennial Kingdom. Perhaps the best point that can be made is that the Church will experience the Millennial Kingdom firsthand and will participate in it. We do not need to take Israel's place to have an important role in Christ's rule. It is the most splendid task of all, just being His Bride and pointing others to Him so that the world may bring Him worship and glory. If only we would be faithful to that task today.

CHAPTER 10
THE BELIEVER AND THE GREAT WHITE THRONE JUDGMENT

No one enjoys the prospect of judgment, especially if it pertains to them. At first glance, the title of this chapter would naturally be a cause for concern. The Biblical teaching about the Great White Throne Judgment is frightful. The reality is that there will be a future judgment, and that judgment will be horrific for those who are judged in it. The verdict and sentence are dreadful beyond words. John records the event in Revelation 20:

> Then I saw a great white throne and Him who sat upon it, from whose presence earth and heaven fled away, and no place was found for them. And I saw the dead, the great and the small, standing before the throne, and books were opened; and another book was opened, which is *the book* of life; and the dead were judged from the things which were written in the books, according to their deeds. And the sea gave up the dead which were in it, and death and Hades gave up the dead which were in them; and they were judged, every one *of them* according to their deeds. Then death and Hades were thrown into the lake of fire. This is the second death, the lake of fire. And if anyone's name was not found written in the book of life, he was thrown into the lake of fire (Revelation 20:11-15).

A question must come to mind, "In what way is the Believer linked to this judgment?" After all, the Bible teaches that "there is now no condemnation for those who are in Christ Jesus" (Romans 8:1). An earlier chapter also confirmed that the judgments of the Tribulation are not designed for the Believer. In fact, the Believer will not even be present on the earth at that time. These things are true, but they do not prevent us from viewing the ultimate judgments upon the unbeliever. For those who would prefer their future after death to simply be relaxing in a hammock with a glass of lemonade, this chapter will not be pleasant. Yet, I believe that it is important that the Believer be present at this great judgment.

Reaching this point in the study of the future experiences of the Believer, I have purposely walked you chronologically through what the Bible teaches. I have also intentionally bypassed the events of the Tribulation period and the career of the antichrist during those seven years when the Believer will be in Heaven. I have addressed the only judgment that pertains to the Believer, the reward ceremony. It is not a judgment to see if we belong in Heaven, but it will test our service to Christ and determine what has value. Chronologically, it is logical that Believers will not face a judgment to determine their future, because of the Marriage of the Lamb and the promises that Christ and the Believer will never be separated. The key principle about Believers is that they will always be with the Lord. When He comes at the Second Coming to this Earth, the Believers will come with Him. When He sets up and governs the Earth during the Millennial Reign, the Believers will reign with Him. Logically then, when Christ judges at the Great White Throne, the Believers must be present with Him.

For a few moments, I would like to take us off our course and mention a few things that are significant to the future. As Believers, we discuss the Rapture often, sometimes as if it were the only thing important in the end times. Scripture, however, does mention other resurrections, some directly and some indirectly. This is true concerning the Old Testament saints just prior to the Millennial Kingdom. They will be seen alive on the Earth to receive the literal promises of the Land and the Kingdom that God has spoken to them (Daniel 12). I believe that the Tribulational saints will also be resurrected and placed within glorified bodies just prior to the Millennial Kingdom so that they may reign with Christ (Revelation 20:4). It would appear that sometime around the time of these resurrections, there must be a judgment for these, probably similar to the Believer's judgment regarding rewards for service.

One more resurrection concerning saints might be considered, though there are questions that have no direct answers. It appears that there must be a resurrection for Millennial saints, assuming that there will be saints who will die during that time. I am not aware that the Bible teaches that saints cannot die during the Millennium, only that it will seem out of place for one to die before the age of 100 (Isaiah 65:20). Should death continue, then resurrection will be necessary. Therefore, shortly after the Millennium is complete, all Believers (Old Testament,

Tribulational, and Millennial saints) will be resurrected, in addition to the Church Age Believers this book concerns.

Now as for the rest of the world, the unsaved (non-believers), both from Old Testament and New Testament times, will have their resurrection. This group will include every unbeliever from Creation to the end of the Millennial Kingdom. Since they will have died without faith, they will be placed in a place called Hades or Hell as a temporary holding place until the final judgment at the Great White Throne. Considering all the people who have lived on this earth since the day of creation, I am afraid there is an incredible number of people in that place waiting their judgment day.

While I am off course, it is best to explain the difference between Hell and the Lake of Fire. Often people speak as if they are the same. Rather, their differences can be compared to some degree to the difference between jail and prison. Our system for those who are arrested includes the basic idea that one may spend time in jail as they await their day in court, and if convicted, they will be moved to a permanent location in prison to serve their sentence. Hell is a temporary location for restraint and torment for the unbeliever. There, they wait for their judgment day. Their sentence will include a permanent residence in the Lake of Fire.

Revelation 19 and 20 describe a series of horrible judgments that will take place. The first one mentioned is the judgment of the antichrist and the false prophet:

> And the beast (antichrist) was seized, and with him the false prophet who performed the signs in his presence, by which he deceived those who had received the mark of the beast and those who worshiped his image; these two were thrown alive into the lake of fire which burns with brimstone (Revelation 19:20).

These two will be the first occupants of the Lake of Fire. It is interesting to note that they will not be included in the Great White Throne Judgment.

Following these a thousand years later, Satan himself will be judged and thrown into the Lake of Fire. Revelation 20:10 states, "And the devil who deceived them was thrown into the lake of fire and brimstone, where the beast and the false prophet are also; and they will be tormented day and night forever and ever." Here we see that Satan is not the caretaker of the Lake of Fire. Our cartoonists have done a disservice in portraying Satan and his demons as the supervisors of torment. Rather, the Bible shows that they will be tormented, too. It is worth stating that the Lake of Fire does not annihilate or consume or even render unconscious its occupants. When Satan is cast into it (and I think the demons as well at this time), the antichrist and the false prophet are still alive and still being tormented.

A third judgment involves the present Earth and Heaven. As I have expressed, the time we will actually spend in the present Heaven is limited. The Believer will depart from Heaven either by death or by the Rapture. After the seven year Tribulation, the Believer will come back to the Earth to dwell with Christ during the Millennial Kingdom. I do not find that we will return to the present Heaven. John states that at the time of the Great White Throne Judgment, the present Earth and present Heaven will flee away and no place will be found for them (Revelation 20:11). This coming event has been written about multiple times in Scripture. Isaiah recorded, 'Lift up your eyes to the sky, Then look to the earth beneath; For the sky will vanish like smoke, And the earth will wear out like a garment" (Isaiah 51:6). Peter also stated, 'But by His word the present heavens and earth are being reserved for fire, kept for the day of judgment and destruction of ungodly men" (2 Peter 3:7). He also wrote, "But the day of the Lord will come like a thief, in which the heavens will pass away with a roar and the elements will be destroyed with intense heat, and the earth and its works will be burned up" (2 Peter 3:10). The description of this event suggests that the present Earth and Heaven will be dissolved, not reconditioned. The reality of it is not beyond the power of God. As Scripture shows us, He is capable of speaking a word to bring the Earth and Heaven into existence. He is also the One who will bring about their destruction. No atomic weapons will be necessary to accomplish this, nor will man get the credit. It is my belief that God's Word should be taken literally, and the destruction of the present Earth and Heaven must be literal as well. This will certainly concrete the fact that there will be no place to hide from the presence of the Lord.

One final judgment is mentioned in these two chapters of Revelation (19-20) and it is the judgment this chapter concerns. It is the Great White Throne Judgment and it pertains to the unbelievers. They will be resurrected and brought before the judgment seat of Christ. The reality of the moment will not suggest that they still have any hope of reversing their future. For those who have already spent many years in Hell, they were not reformed nor did they have a change of heart. Jesus often mentioned that it was a place of gnashing of teeth. Revelation 20 does not give them a second chance, as some mistakenly suppose. John states, "And I saw the dead, the great and the small, standing before the throne, and books were opened; and another book was opened, which is the book of life; and the dead were judged from the things which were written in the books, according to their deeds" (Revelation 20:12). Added to this is the fact that there is no place left for them besides the Lake of Fire. The present Heaven is gone. The present Earth is gone. Even Death and Hades (Hell) is gone. "Then death and Hades were thrown into the lake of fire. This is the second death, the lake of fire" (Revelation 20:14). The only location left for them is the Lake of Fire.

The fact that they are judged by their works shows that faith is nonexistent in their case and their deeds do not measure up to God's standard. Yet, the final determination will be that they did not believe in the Lord. "And if anyone's name was not found written in the book of life, he was thrown into the lake of fire" (Revelation 20:15). The end result is eternal separation from God. It is frightful and forever.

Now, what does that have to do with the Church Age Believer? First of all, we will be with the Lord. Where He is, there we will be as well. When He judges at the Great White Throne, we will be present. There will not be any other location for us to go to, nor any other thing to busy ourselves with. We shall witness this judgment. It is just as important that we see the justice and righteousness of our Lord as it is for the unbeliever. Jesus has been given the authority to judge by His Father and before Him every knee will bow and every tongue will confess that He is Lord. Our place is to give Him glory, and this judgment will highlight His glory in the midst of the unrighteous. Our presence there is to worship our Savior and Lord. We are everlasting testimonies of the difference God's grace makes. Paul stated that "in the ages to come He might show the surpassing riches of His grace in kindness toward us in Christ Jesus" (Ephesians 2:7). It will be quite evident on that day.

In addition to this, the fact that we are present will be further condemnation to those who did not believe. The unbeliever will not have the ability to say that God did not give them a chance. As Paul wrote:

> But thanks be to God, who always leads us in triumph in Christ, and manifests through us the sweet aroma of the knowledge of Him in every place. For we are a fragrance of Christ to God among those who are being saved and among those who are perishing; to the one an aroma from death to death, to the other an aroma from life to life (2 Corinthians 2:14-16).

What a motivation for missions and evangelism we currently have, to declare the excellencies of Him who called us out of darkness! Though we will continue to be witnesses of the same on that day, the unbeliever will be condemned by the very fact that they did not believe the message of truth.

Of all the events that the Believer will experience in the future, I do not hesitate to think that this judgment will be the most difficult to view. It will not change our relationship with our Lord, but I do think it will add to the praises we will shout before His throne. Even with all that said, there are still great events yet to discuss about the Believer's future.

CHAPTER 11
THE BELIEVER AND THE NEW HEAVEN AND NEW EARTH

When I started writing this book, I said I was like a tour guide for a place I have never been. In a sense, this is a good thing. It forces me to depend completely on the Word of God for my instruction. Experience and speculation are poor substitutes. There are several stories being circulated and popularized about those who have died, entered Heaven and have returned to tell us about it. Personally, I do not need their testimony to convince me that Heaven is real. It is not necessary for extra-biblical support to strengthen my faith. However, I think that the messages we receive from these 'heavenly visits' ought to be set next to the revealed truth of God's Word. One single contradiction nullifies the truthfulness of it all. It has been pointed out that some of the stories have no comments about Jesus in them. Yet, there are many reports of Heaven's description. Here is where confusion usually sets in and there is a very good reason for it. The fact is that assumptions are made about Heaven's appearance simply on a piece or two of Bible verses. We have heard of those who have entered 'the pearly gates' and we sing songs about the streets of gold. Yet, these are descriptions of the future Heaven, not the present Heaven. The future Heaven (or New Heaven, as the Bible calls it) is a place that no one can say they have visited. Those who claim to have gone there have done something miraculous since the New Heaven does not exist yet. When I was young, it seemed to be the goal we had as children to be the first ones to stomp in the yard of new-fallen snow. I do not believe my mother had the opportunity to take a picture of a beautiful winter scene without the appearance that a troop of soldiers had passed by on it. The Heaven I write about in this chapter has never been 'stomped' through by visitors. You will not find their footprints on the streets of gold, nor their fingerprints on the pearly gates.

At this point in our study, you have been made aware that there are two different places called Heaven. The first place is the present Heaven. The Bible identifies it as the place where God's throne is. It has the true temple in it. It has an emerald rainbow around the throne. It has a sea of glass. It has many rooms in it – places prepared for us by Christ. Added to them are some interesting details that spark my imagination. Job 38 speaks about the storehouse of snow and the storehouse of hail. Deuteronomy 28 tells of a storehouse of rain in heaven. I wonder if it would be accurate to picture rooms in Heaven that have door labels that read, "Snow," "Rain," or "Hail?" I cannot say definitely. However, what I do note is that our description of the present Heaven is limited. Our stay in the present Heaven will be limited, too. If the Rapture should occur today, Believers will go to the present Heaven to reside for seven years. Those will be busy years with award and wedding ceremonies. Then, the Believer will return to the Earth with Christ as He rules for 1000 years in Jerusalem. Remember, no matter where Christ is, we will always be with Him. At the conclusion of the Millennial Reign, the present Heaven and present Earth will flee from the presence (face) of the Lord and will be seen no more. Then the time will come for the Lord to fulfill the remainder of His promises about the New Heaven and New Earth. The details are found predominantly in Revelation 21 and 22.

    This chapter brings us to the final destination for the Believer. Two themes are addressed in Revelation 21 by John, the Believer and the presence of God and the Believer and the city of God. Both of the themes highlight the idea of "new." For starters, the Believer will experience a new residence. John writes, "Then I saw a new heaven and a new earth; for the first heaven and the first earth passed away, and there is no longer *any* sea" (Revelation 21:1). There is debate in the commentaries about the meaning of 'new.' It cannot mean refurbished, remodeled, renovated, reconditioned, revamped, restored, repaired, or renewed. Rather it means unused. If God had meant for the verse to say 'renewed,' He had the Greek preposition available to Him to put in front of the word 'new' to make it 'renewed.' He had used it before when He instructed Paul to write in the letters to the Ephesians and the Colossians. There it is found that we are being 'renewed' into the image of Christ. God could have used the same word in Revelation 21, but He did not. His promise is a New Heaven and a New Earth. Three times He specifically states it in relation to the removal of the old Heaven and Earth. In Isaiah 65:17 we read, "For behold, I create new heavens and a new earth; And the former things will not be remembered or come to mind." It is interesting to note that the word "create" is the same word found in Genesis 1:1. Isaiah 66:22 adds, "For just as the new heavens and the new earth Which I make will endure before Me," declares the LORD, "So your offspring and your name will endure." In the New Testament, Peter writes on the same theme:

> But the day of the Lord will come like a thief, in which the heavens will pass away with a roar and the elements will be destroyed with intense heat, and the earth and its works will be burned up. Since all these things are to be destroyed in this way, what sort of people ought you to be in holy conduct and godliness, looking for and hastening the coming of the day of God, because of which the heavens will be destroyed by burning, and the elements will melt with intense heat! But according to His promise we are looking for new heavens and a new earth, in which righteousness dwells (2 Peter 3:10-13).

Related to the 'new' is the fact that the 'old' is done away with. Peter states that they will be burned up. Isaiah mentioned that the former troubles will be forgotten (Isaiah 65:16) and the former things will not be remembered (Isaiah 65:17). There is a nice advantage to things being new. The results will bring in a gladness and rejoicing, 'for behold, I create Jerusalem for rejoicing and her people for gladness" (Isaiah 65:18).

Besides being new, the future Heaven and Earth will also be forever. When God promised that His people, the Jews, will be an offspring which will endure, He based it on the fact that the New Heavens and the New Earth will endure forever. For either one of them to not endure eliminates the integrity of His promise. Such a promise is not made about the present Heaven or present Earth. In several instances, they are referred to as 'passing away.' Therefore, our new residence will have an enduring quality that our present residence does not. A contrast is also found in the fact that the New Heaven and New Earth will be known for a place where righteousness dwells (2 Peter 3:13). We cannot say that is true of our present residence. The New Heaven, in contrast, will have the characteristics of former things being forgotten, a quality of endurance, and a place where righteousness will dwell. The only other description given in Revelation 21:1 of the New Heaven and Earth is that there will be no sea. It is amazing that the Bible does not go into much description of the New Heaven and Earth. From the verses that shall be mentioned in the rest of this chapter, a few assumptions may be drawn to help explain the purpose of the New Heaven and Earth. They will exist for a place for man to dwell and God to dwell with them (Revelation 21:3). Specifically, the Earth will be a place for the nations (Revelation 21:26). It could very well be the fulfillment of the promises that the Lord gave to the meek ("Blessed are the gentle ['meek'] for they will inherit the earth" (Matthew 5:5). Plus, the promise to Abraham included an everlasting residence in the land God gave to him. I cannot say exactly how this shall be fulfilled, but I do understand it to be a literal promise and that the Earth must exist for it to be realized. Therefore, I assume that the New Earth will be populated with the Believers who have entered the eternal state and have been divided into their national identities.

Another location of residence is described in Revelation 21. Properly, it is called the New Jerusalem. It is not the New Earth nor the New Heaven. John gives us a great deal of description about it. Often that description is mistakenly applied to the present Heaven. Rather, the New Jerusalem is a location all to itself. It is called 'the holy city' and is seen 'coming down out of heaven' in Revelation 21:2. It is very fitting that it be called the New Jerusalem. Just as the promise to Abraham is everlasting, so is the promise to David. In 2 Samuel 7:16, the Lord told David, "your house and your kingdom shall endure before Me forever; your throne shall be established forever." A key to the promise is the location of the throne in Jerusalem. With the old Jerusalem being destroyed with the rest of the Earth, it makes sense that a New Jerusalem must be created to complete the promise and locate the throne of David. As before, the city is called the "New Jerusalem." It is not a renovated or reconditioned Jerusalem.

The present Jerusalem has quite a history. Originally it was a city of the Jebusites – a Canaanite nation that needed to be removed from the land promised to Israel. It was captured by King David and made into his royal city. It was the location of the Temple. It was also the city in which Jesus was crucified. Terrible sinners lived in it and terrible events took place in it. It has not always been associated with good things. It stands to reason that if the Heavens will be new and the Earth will be new, then Jerusalem will also need to be new and the promises of God are not invalidated.

It is interesting to note that a new kind of dwelling relationship will also exist between God and man. We are mindful of the fact that in the original creation, man was made to dwell on Earth. There, God could have fellowship with man, but it was always God coming to man. Man broke the fellowship by sinning. In God's perfect plan, His Son came to the Earth at His first coming. We read of His life, death, resurrection and ascension to Heaven in the Gospels. We also read of His promise that He would prepare a place for us so that He can take us to be with Him. All of these things involved the present Earth and present Heaven. But what makes the New Earth and Heaven unique is that the dwelling of God will be with man. It will not be a matter of Him coming to us or us going to be with Him. Rather, we shall share in the new dwelling place, much like a brand new house that no one has occupied. The New Heaven and Earth is a place where no one has dwelt before. It is 'unused.' Therefore it will be a common place for us to share with God, for it will be a new dwelling location for Him as well. Revelation 21:3 states, "And I heard a loud voice from the throne, saying, 'Behold, the tabernacle of God is among men, and He will dwell among them, and they shall be His people, and God Himself will be among them.'" I cannot fully explain such a thing. In our present world, there is a fear that should we see God, we will not live. Manoah had that fear in Judges 13. But such a fear will not exist in our new residence. We shall dwell with God.

Just think of the new experiences that will follow. I believe they are so 'new' to us that the best way to describe them is in the negative. John writes, "and He will wipe away every tear from their eyes; and there will no longer be *any* death; there will no longer be *any* mourning, or crying, or pain; the first things have passed away" (Revelation 21:4). In their place are all new things. God Himself says, "Behold, I am making all things new" (Revelation 21:5). A fitting situation this will be. In our new residence we shall have a new experience of dwelling with God forever. This will be the most profound experience we will know. With all the interest in seeing the place, how often do we give attention to the fact that we shall be with Him?

While I am discussing the New Heaven and Earth, we should take a tour of the New Jerusalem. Much of the two concluding chapters of Revelation give a description of the holy city. I stress, as the Bible does, that it is a separate location from the New Heaven and the New Earth. The New Heaven is mentioned in Revelation 21:1, but it is not described. The New Earth is also mentioned in verse 1, and its description is basically that it will have no sea. In much more detail, the New Jerusalem is seen as coming down from Heaven (Revelation 21:2). It is described as having a brilliant appearance as the glory of God (Revelation 21:11). As to its particular descriptions, John describes its walls as having the height of a 20 story building (Revelation 21:17). They are fifteen hundred miles in length and width – an enormous distance that spans from North Dakota to Southern Texas. They are made entirely of jasper. We are told that there are three gates on each wall (north, south, east, and west). Each gate is made of a single pearl and the streets are made of pure gold (Revelation 21:12-15, 21). The city walls are built upon twelve foundation stones with incredible and beautiful descriptions (Revelation 21:14, 19-20). The beauty of such a place is staggering to the imagination. It is no wonder that the city is described as a bride prepared for her husband.

Added to its description are the things that will not be necessary in the city. There will be no temple in the New Jerusalem because "the Lord God the Almighty and the Lamb are its temple" (Revelation 21:22). There will be no need of sunshine or the beam of the moon, "for the glory of God has illumined it, and its lamp is the Lamb."

The relationship of the New Jerusalem to the New Earth is quite interesting. When describing the New Jerusalem, Revelation 21 highlights the fact that the gates of the city will never be closed (Revelation 21:24). The nations and the kings of the earth will walk by the light of the city and there will be no night time (Revelation 21:24-25). These same nations and kings will bring their glory and honor into the city, I assume for the purpose of worshipping the Lord. Since the New Heaven and Earth will be characterized as a place where righteousness dwells, it is fitting to state that nothing unclean will ever enter the New Jerusalem (Revelation 21:27). All that will occupy the New Earth, the New Heaven and the New Jerusalem will be identified as holy to the Lord. Nations of Believers will regularly attend worship of the Lord in the New Jerusalem. These things are quite beyond our experience and knowledge in this present Earth, but they are the things that God has prepared for those who love Him (1 Corinthians 2:9). I think it is proper for us to be fascinated by the description that God has given to us of our future dwelling place. No doubt, the realization of it will far surpass our human attempts to understand it from here.

Our study has followed the chronological aspects of the Believer and Heaven, and has brought us to our final location. Yet, there is one more part of our future that I will discuss in the final chapter. Often it is asked, "what will we do up there?" It is best that we know since it will be our everlasting occupation.

CHAPTER 12
THE BELIEVER AND ETERNITY

We live in a society that changes often and it is difficult for us to comprehend the concept of forever. I do not believe that our limited minds can grasp something that is unending. As Paul wrote, "For now we see in a mirror dimly…" (1 Corinthians 13:12). The concept is not exactly a foggy view; it is a limited view. The best observations we have are of those who are seeing life through a broken fragment of a mirror. It is no wonder that the vastness of forever exceeds our perspective.

Our study has brought us to a final look at the Believer's future as a citizen of Heaven. Each aspect of it will be dominated by the term forever. Our occupancy of the New Heaven and Earth will be forever. I assume that we will be capable of transporting from one location to another. Our service to the Lord will also be forever. No longer will the limitations of this current life prevent us from serving Him with all our heart, soul, strength and might. A teenager once asked me the question, "Will we get bored doing the same thing forever?" I doubt that such a thought will enter our minds there. Who would want things to change when they are the best? What could possibly exceed the finest and greatest arrangement of being with Christ forever?

As John describes in Revelation 22 the glories of the New Jerusalem, he mentions a river and a tree. The river is identified as "the water of life" and is proceeding from the actual throne of God and down the middle of the street (Revelation 22:1). Since God is its source, it will never run dry and the life it represents will never come to an end. All the things that have made life unbearable and limited will be removed. Death will be gone, as well as sickness, pain, sin, and the effects of the curse. These are the things that we understand in our present situation. As we have seen, it is typical to describe our new residence in terms of what will not be there. Yet, in a positive sense, John also tells us what will be there. First of all, we will enjoy the provisions of the water of life. In Revelation 21:6 the Lord said, "I will give to the one who thirsts from the spring of the water of life without cost." And Revelation 22:17 adds, "And let the one who is thirsty come; let the one who wishes take the water of life without cost." I would say that since the Lord often makes reference to the water of life, it must be significant for us. I cannot fully comprehend how "thirst" is part of the picture, except that it will be a consuming desire on our part to partake of such a wonderful thing. However, the great value it has will be understood when we get there. No doubt we shall drink from this water.

Much like the water, we will also partake of the fruit from the Tree of life. Revelation 22:2 tells us of the Tree of Life which bears twelve kinds of fruit every month. Since it is called "the" Tree of Life, I believe that it would be the same tree that was present in the Garden of Eden. We remember that there were two trees actually named in the Genesis account: the Tree of the Knowledge of Good and Evil and the Tree of Life. Concerning the Tree of Life, God had Adam and Eve barred from the garden after their sin to prevent them from taking from the Tree of Life and living forever (Genesis 3:22). At another time, Jesus promised in Revelation 2:7 'To him who overcomes, I will grant to eat of the tree of life which is in the Paradise of God." Now, in Revelation 22:14 He gives the right to the Tree of Life to those who have washed their robes and enter by the gates into the city. Much like the water mentioned before, the significance and value of this is beyond us, however it is clear that we will have the joy of eating from that Tree. In addition to that, Revelation 22:2 states that the leaves of the tree were for the healing of the nations. Typically, we assume that if healing were necessary, then there must be sickness or injury. However, the word is more closely related to maintenance or service than it is to sickness or disease. Commentaries have attempted to explain this from a limited view. It is interesting that John does not explain it, but merely tells what he sees. Whatever it is meant to convey, it must be in keeping with the fact that there will no longer be any curse (Revelation 22:3). I sense that the water, the fruit of the tree, and the leaves are all meant to be taken and enjoyed. In some fashion they will coincide with our everlasting living arrangements. Certainly, if Christ can partake of food in His resurrected body, it stands to reason that we can and will, too.

A second point John makes concerning our future and forever presence in this place has to do with what we will be doing. The entire focus of the book you are reading is to describe the relationship between Heaven and the Believer. There have been many descriptions given to us for our imaginations to process. Yet, we must come to the big question: "What is the New Heaven and Earth for?" Surely, there must be a purpose, for God always has a purpose for what He does.

I disagree with the modern "Christian" concept that Heaven will be what you want it to be. I have heard the idea that if one cannot live without their cat, Fluffy, and that it will not be Heaven without Fluffy, then Fluffy will be there. Besides the fact that Scripture does not support such a concept, it is obvious that many definitions of Heaven are very man-centered. It is often viewed as simply man's reward for their life down here. It is a celestial giant hammock on a bright summer day under a shade tree and with a cold glass of lemonade. Cartoon depictions typically involve white robes, halos, wings, harps and sitting on clouds. Practically every religion has the concept of Heaven (or Paradise or whatever they seek to name it) being the reward for those who are faithful and worthy in their particular faith. The three dominant themes found in these teachings are pleasure, freedom from distresses, and rewards. Clearly, the Bible has teachings similar to these, however the main point is significantly different. Man-based religions have a man-based eternity. Mankind is the center of the present and the future consideration. On the contrary, the Biblical-based teaching is that we exist for the glory of God and our eternity is a continuance of bringing glory to God. As described in Revelation 22:3, Believers will be called "bond-servants" in that forever place:

> ... and His bond-servants will serve Him; they will see His face, and His name will be on their foreheads. And there will no longer be any night; and they will not have need of the light of a lamp nor the light of the sun, because the Lord God will illumine them; and they will reign forever and ever (Revelation 22:3-5).

A bond-servant is a devoted servant who is entirely at the disposal of his master in a permanent position. In the Old Testament there was a way for a bond-servant to express his devotion to his master by way of an ear piercing (Exodus 21:5-6). The results of the act were to declare that he will be his servant for life. In the New Testament, there are many who are referred to as bond-servants,' including Simeon, Paul, Epaphras, James, and Peter. Their lives were testimonies of their devotion and permanent bond to God, entirely at His disposal and seeking His glory and will. As John highlights in Revelation 22:3-5, the bond-servants are His. They serve Him. They will see His face. His name will be on their foreheads. He will illumine them. The primary focus is on serving Him.

We often sing, "There is joy in serving Jesus" or "the longer I serve Him, the sweeter He grows." We may experience that to some degree down here, but the reality of a service that is forever is what the Bible describes as our future with Him. The things we practice down here, such as praising Him, obeying Him, serving Him, will become a continuous reality in His presence. These are certainly not man-centered or self-centered. The nature of our service will be linked to our worship of Him. The two words, "serve" and "worship" are combined in the thought.

In the Old Testament, we are given much information about the priest in the tabernacle service. They had duties to perform on a daily basis. For example, if a man came to the entrance of the tabernacle with a lamb for sacrifice, it was the priest who would meet him there. After determining the kind of sacrifice the man intended, the priest would slay the lamb by slitting its throat and collecting the blood in a basin. The blood was poured out on the altar. Then, depending upon the type of sacrifice, the body of the animal was skinned and cut up. Some parts were offered as the sacrifice on the altar. Some parts were thrown away. Some parts were reserved for a meal. This same procedure was followed for all who approached to worship the Lord through sacrifice. Imagine what it must have been like the day King Solomon offered up 22,000 oxen and 120,000 sheep! I could only think that for some priests, the act of service became routine. Even though it was an act of worship, I believe it would have been possible to serve without engaging the heart. Even one of the Lord's complaints against the priests in Malachi is that they offered sacrifices not worthy of the Lord.

What a difference it will be when we serve our Lord through worship forever. In eternity, it will be our primary occupation. It will neither be boring nor be a heartless routine. No longer will we need to be encouraged to present our bodies as a living and holy sacrifice, acceptable to God, which is your spiritual service of worship" (Romans 12:1). Not only will our service be continually genuine, but it will have a duration that matches the term forever. John writes, "And there will no longer be *any* night; and they will not have need of the light of a lamp nor the light of the sun, because the Lord God will illumine them…" (Revelation 22:5). Our service will not need to stop due to darkness. No longer will there be a need to sleep because we do not become tired. No longer will we measure 'work' by the clock. Service and worship will have no end. This is where I seek to bring our study to a conclusion. Many of our childhood stories ended with "and they lived happily ever after." Such a phrase hardly does justice to that which the Lord has described to us. In all my efforts to express what the Bible has to say about the Believer's future, I am aware that I fall far short of what the actual experience will provide. Yet, there is a purpose for us knowing these things. They are not merely to satisfy our curiosity. Prophecy has a consistent purpose. Simply put, since these things are so, "what sort of people ought you to be in holy conduct and godliness?" (2 Peter 3:11). Our future has direct ties to our present service and worship of our Lord. We may have limitations, but our hearts and lives ought to be dedicated as bond-servants of Christ in this present world. A true bond-servant does not worry about his future. He has entrusted it to his master. We need not worry about our future either. Our Lord has designed a beautiful forever for us. He has been kind in telling us the different aspects of what our future holds. All of this to encourage us to "be steadfast, immovable, always abounding in the work of the Lord, knowing that your toil is not *in* vain in the Lord" (1 Corinthians 15:58). How practical prophecy is! Since we can read that we shall serve Him forever, we ought to be motivated all the more to be devoted to Him in service today. Since we can read that we shall be like Him, we ought to be prompted to be more like Him each day. The description of Heaven and the Believer ought to affect our hearts and our lives. The last words recorded in Scripture by our Lord are, "Yes, I am coming quickly" (Revelation 22:20).

    Reader, thank you for investing your time in reading this author's limited ability to describe a place I have not seen yet, except through the pages of God's holy Word. I commend you to His Truth, the Bible. It is often said that the eye has not seen and the ear has not heard what God has prepared for those who love Him. But that is not the end of the story. The passage goes on to say:

For to us God revealed *them* through the Spirit; for the Spirit searches all things, even the depths of God. For who among men knows the *thoughts* of a man except the spirit of the man which is in him? Even so the *thoughts* of God no one knows except the Spirit of God. Now we have received, not the spirit of the world, but the Spirit who is from God, so that we may know the things freely given to us by God (1 Corinthians 2:10-12).

As much as I desire that this volume will give you understanding, peace, or comfort; my greater goal is to motivate you to examine God's Word for yourself. Study the Savior who promised, "I will come again and receive you to Myself, that where I am, there you may be also" (John 14:3). "The grace of the Lord Jesus be with all" (Revelation 22:21).

Yale

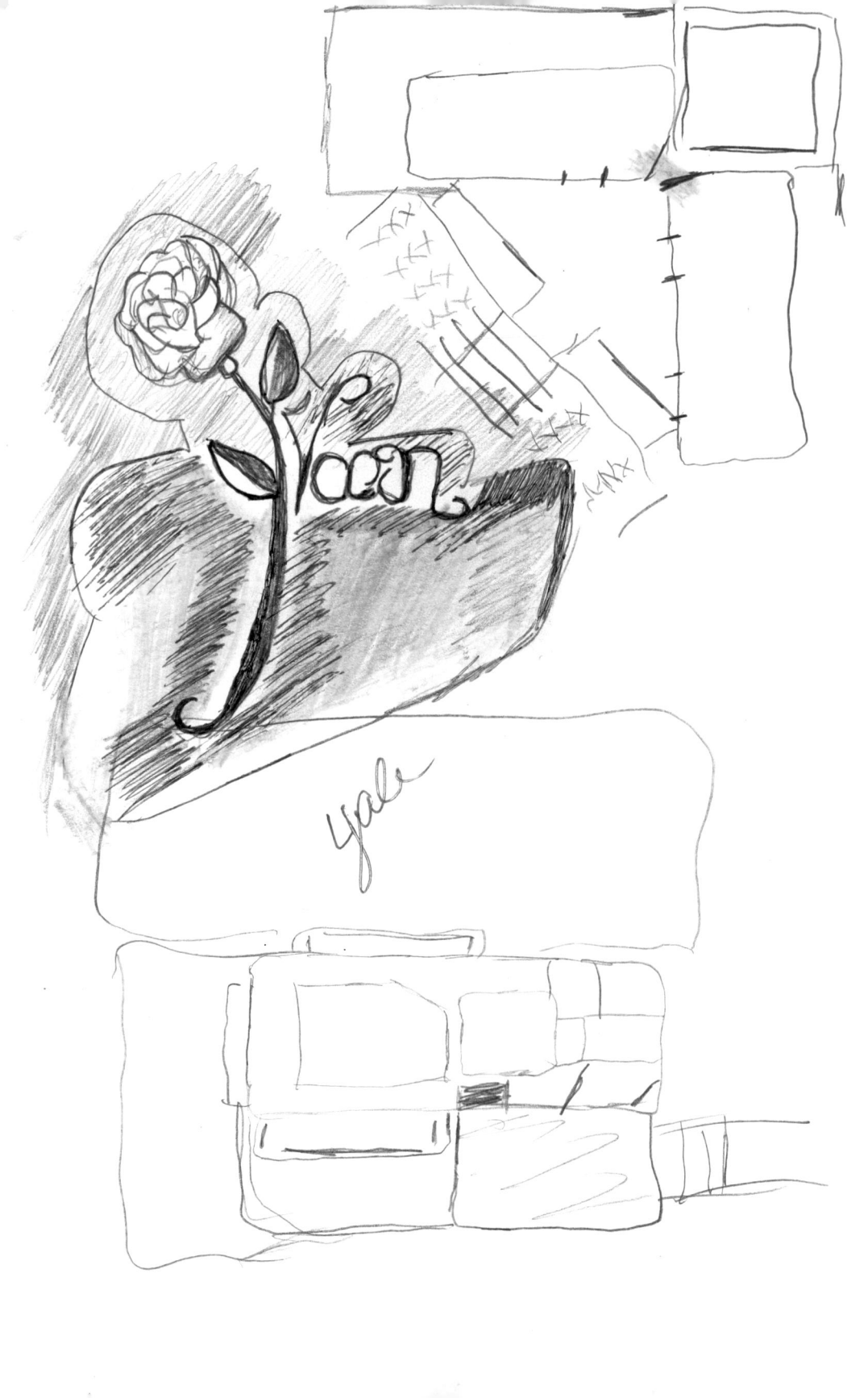